Coloring Books for Grownups
NOH MASKS

VISIT TODAY
ILoveColoringBooksForAdults.com
TO WIN A SET OF PREMIUM COLORED PENCILS

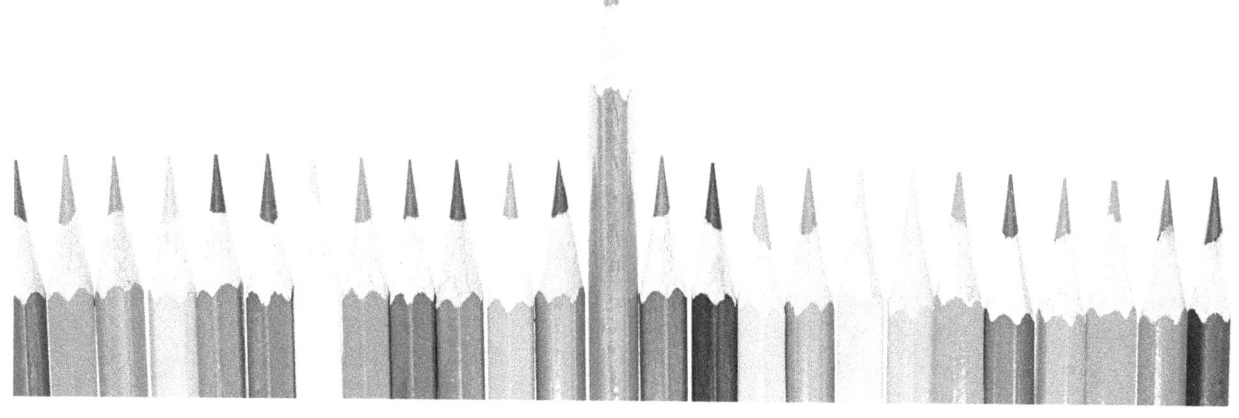

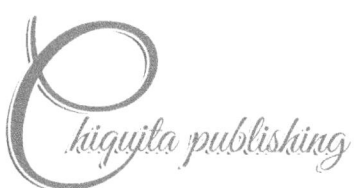
Chiquita publishing

Cover and page design by Cool Journals Studios - Copyright 2015

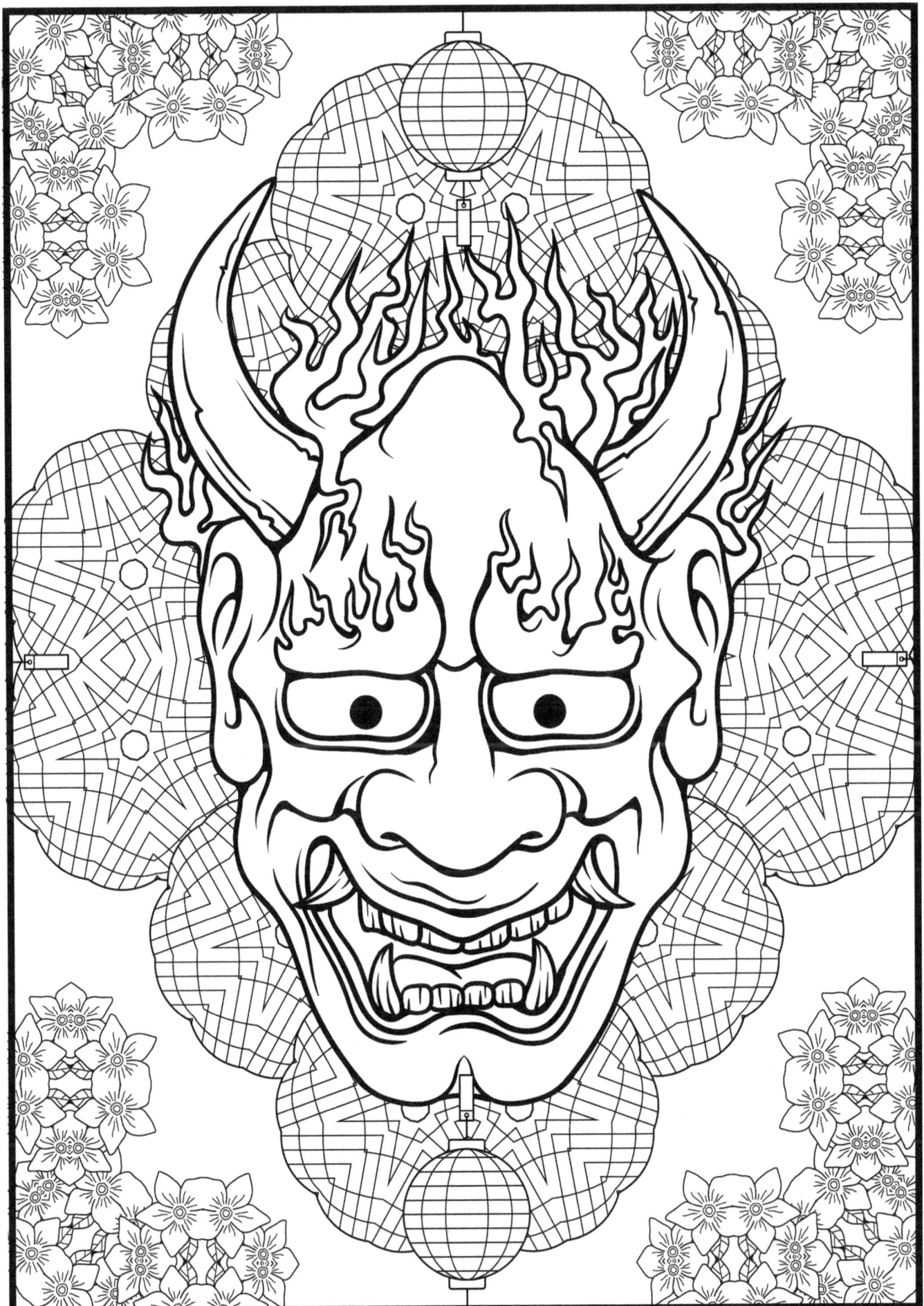

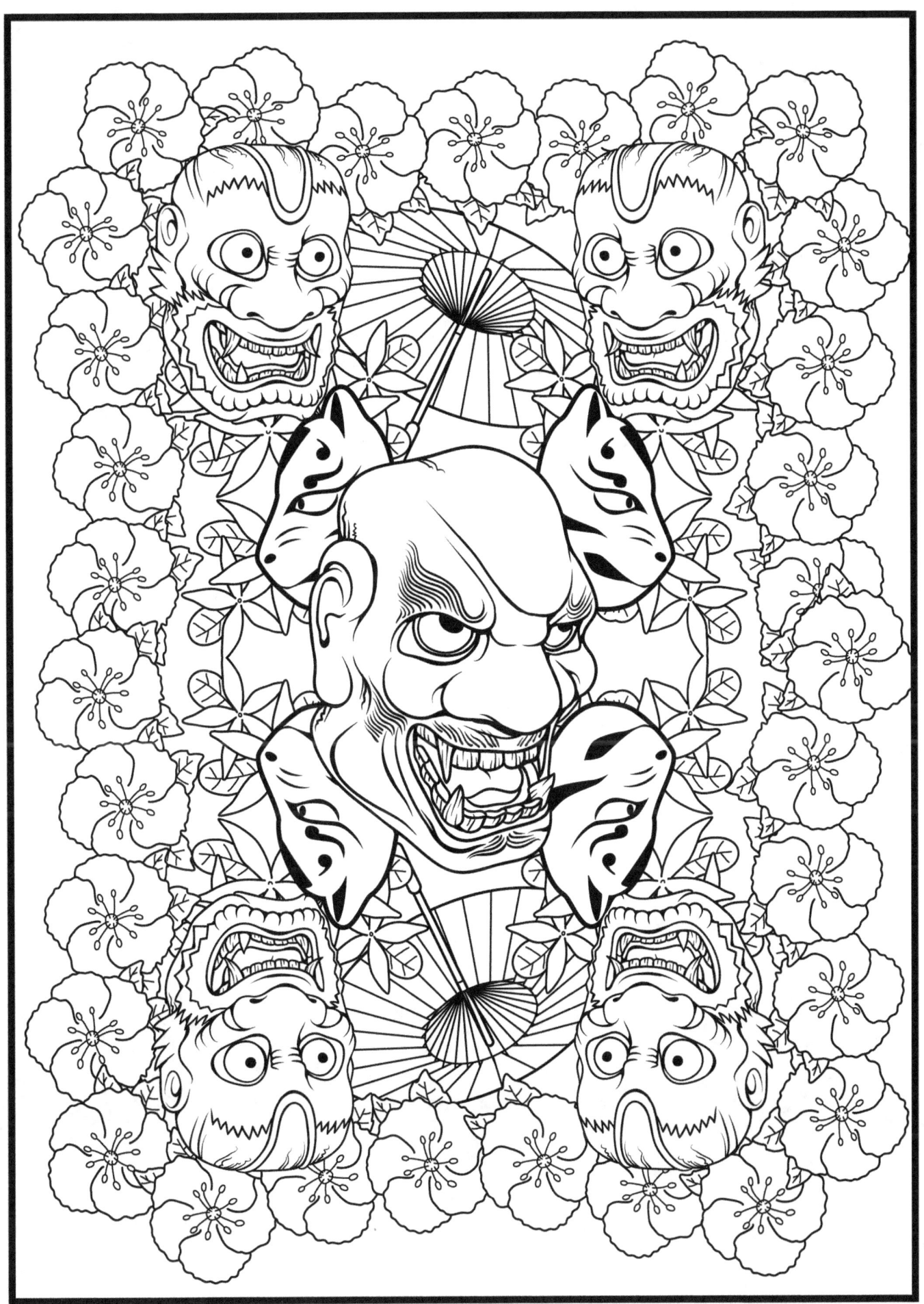

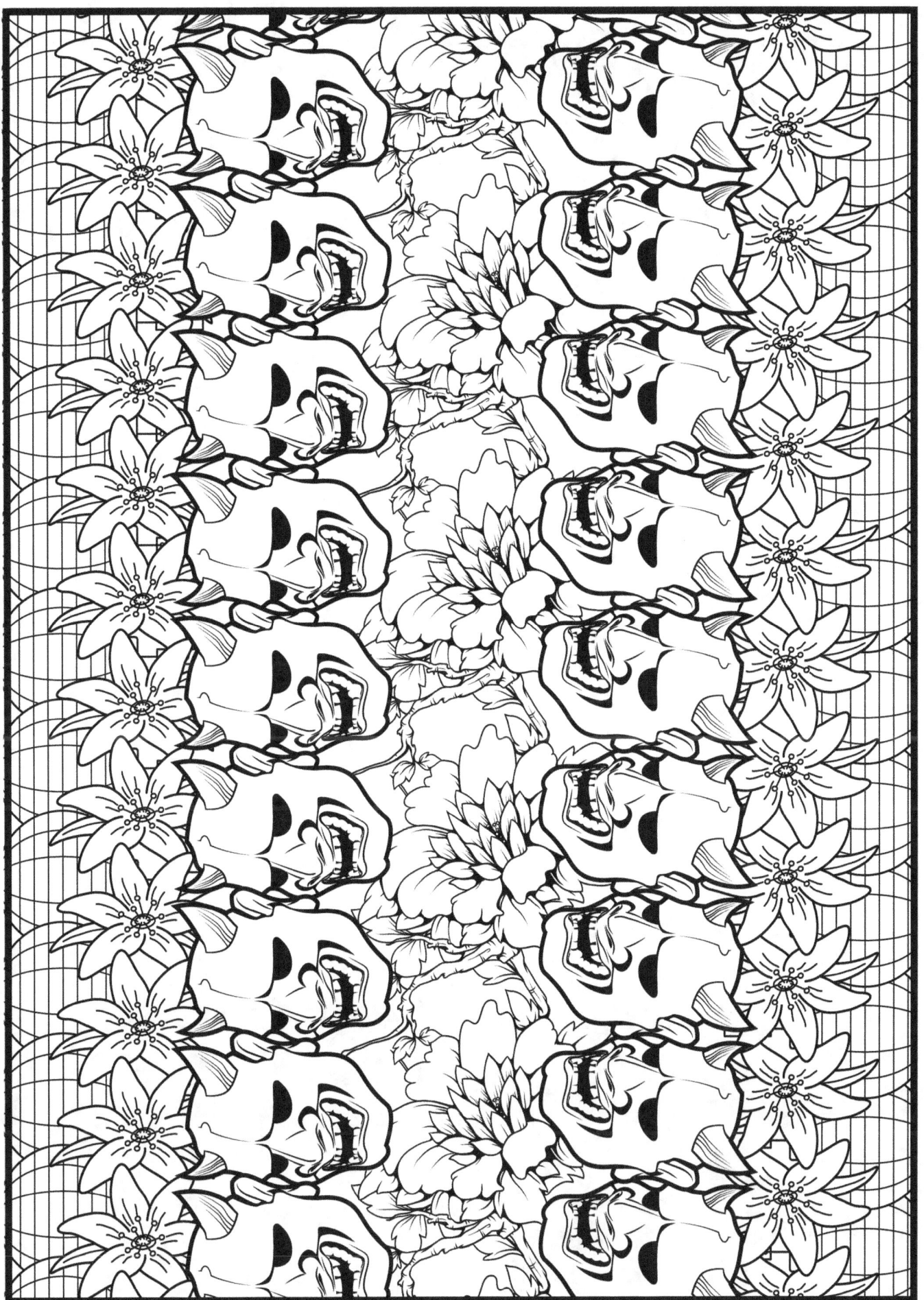

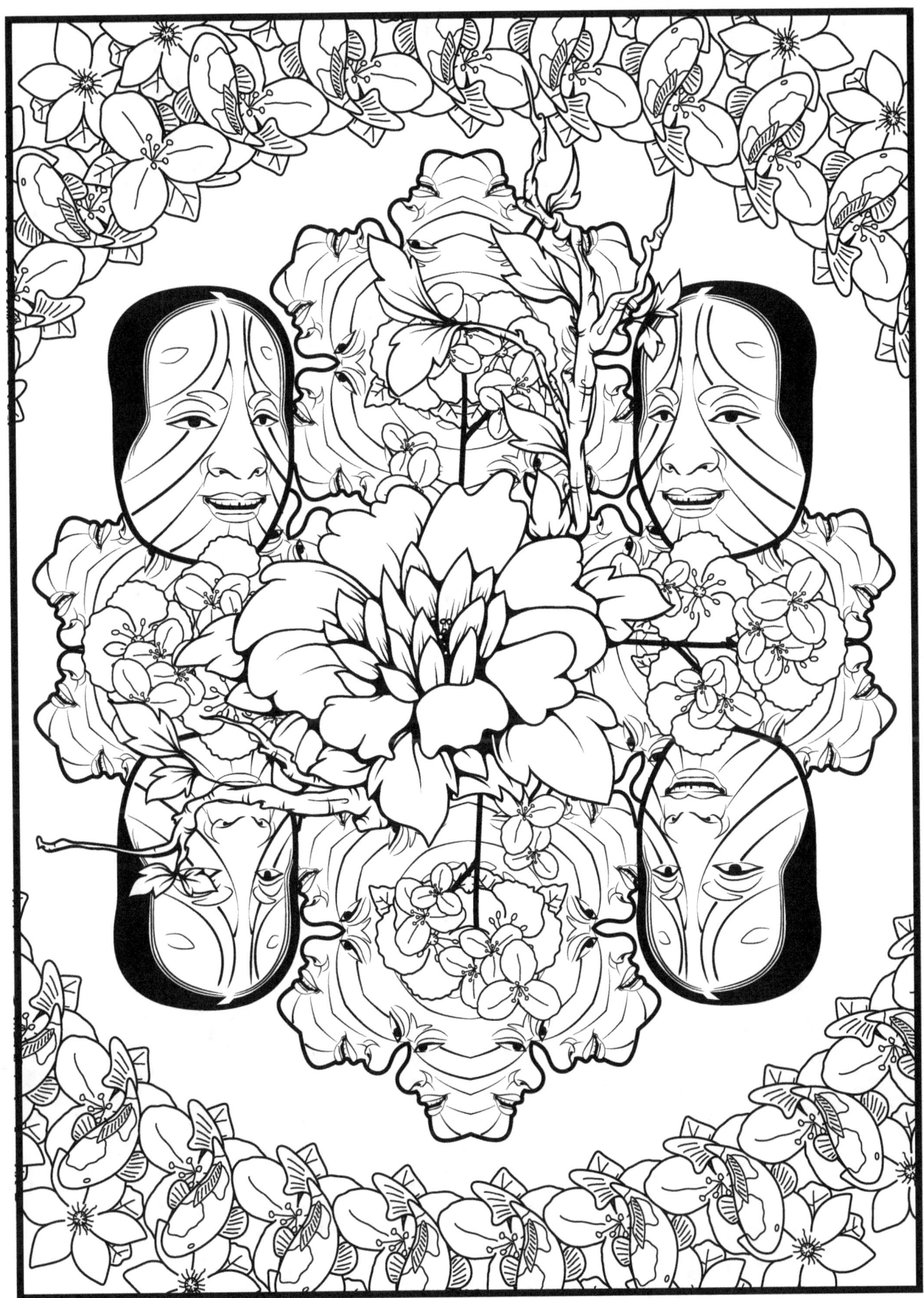

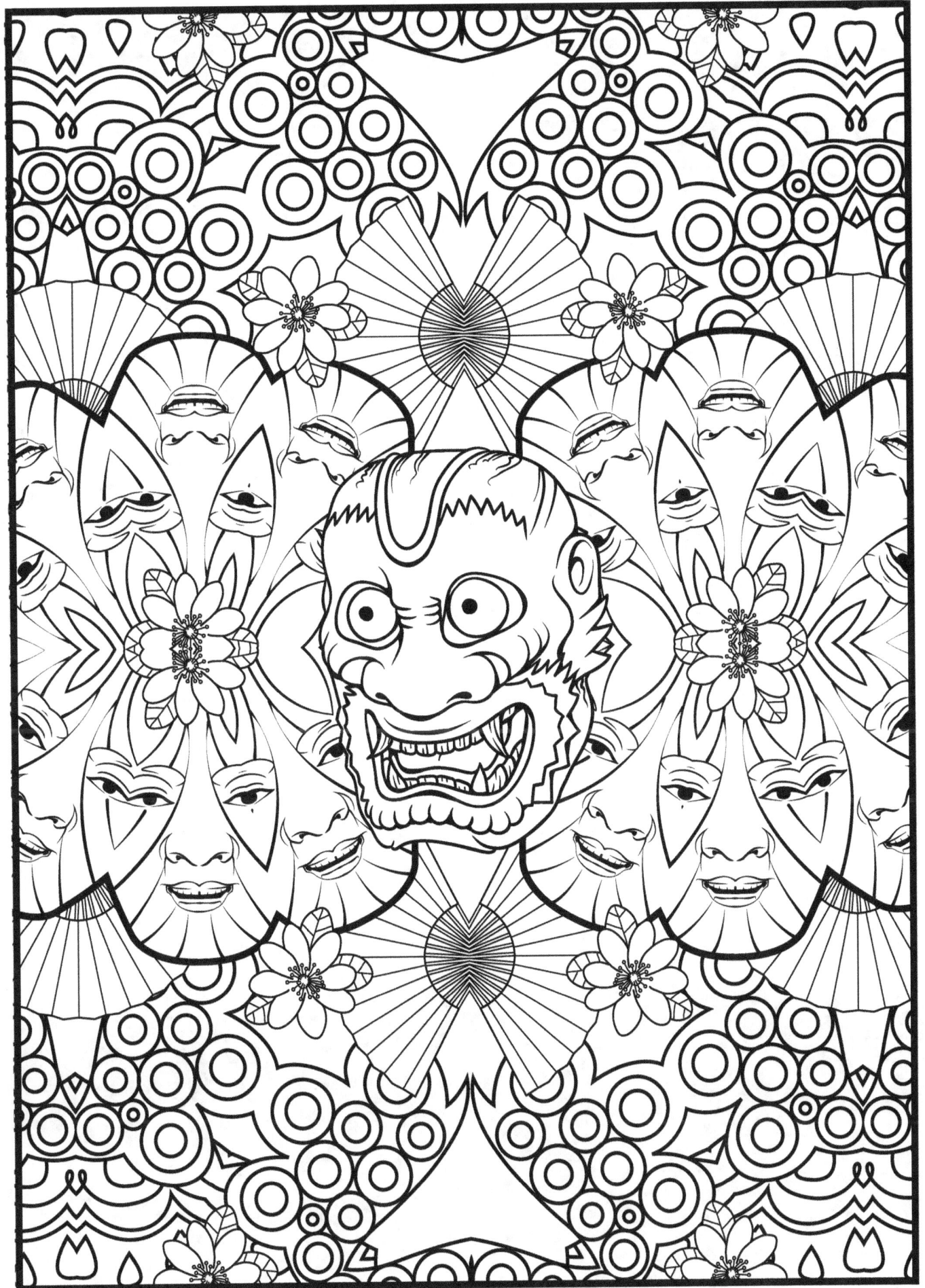

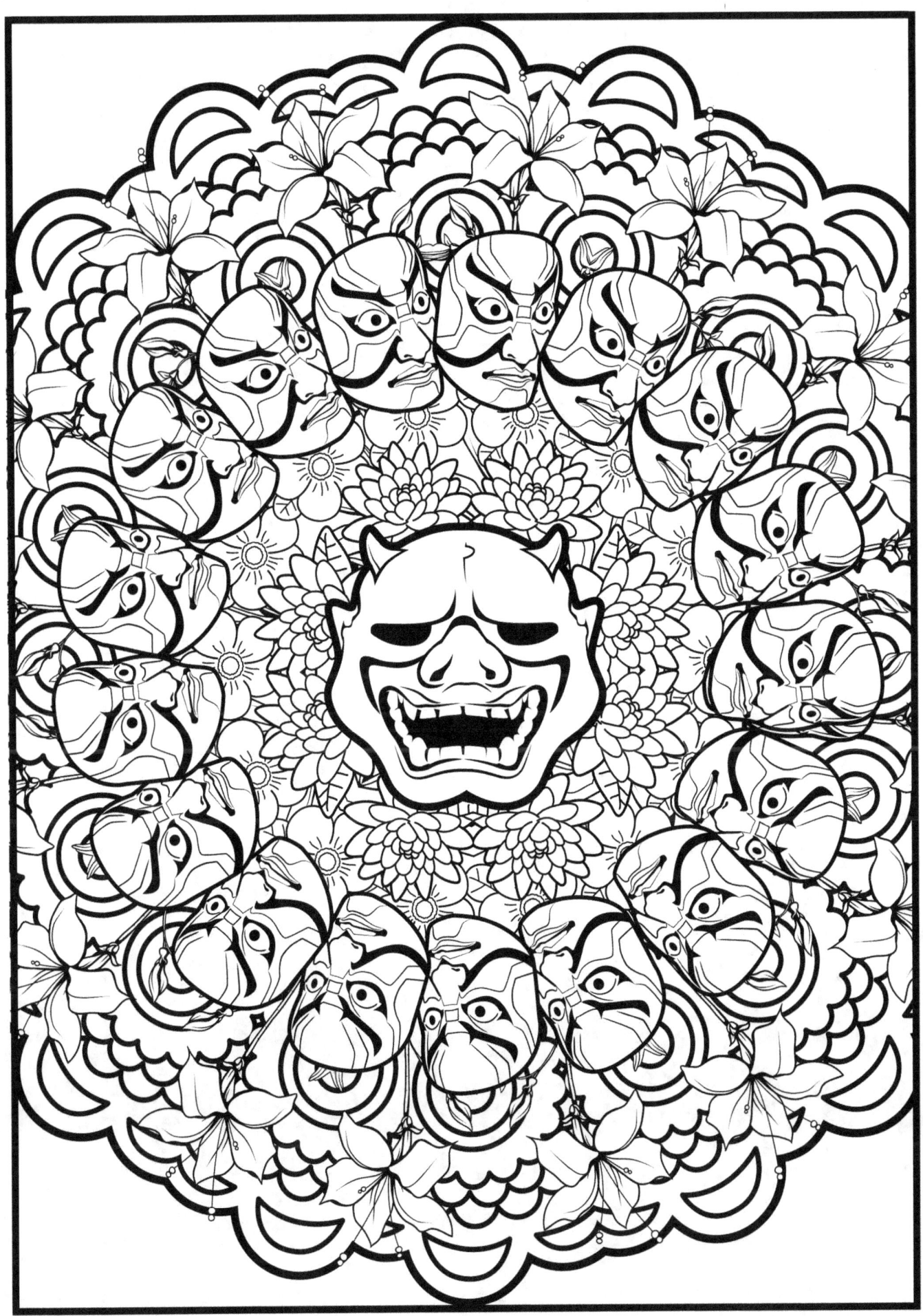

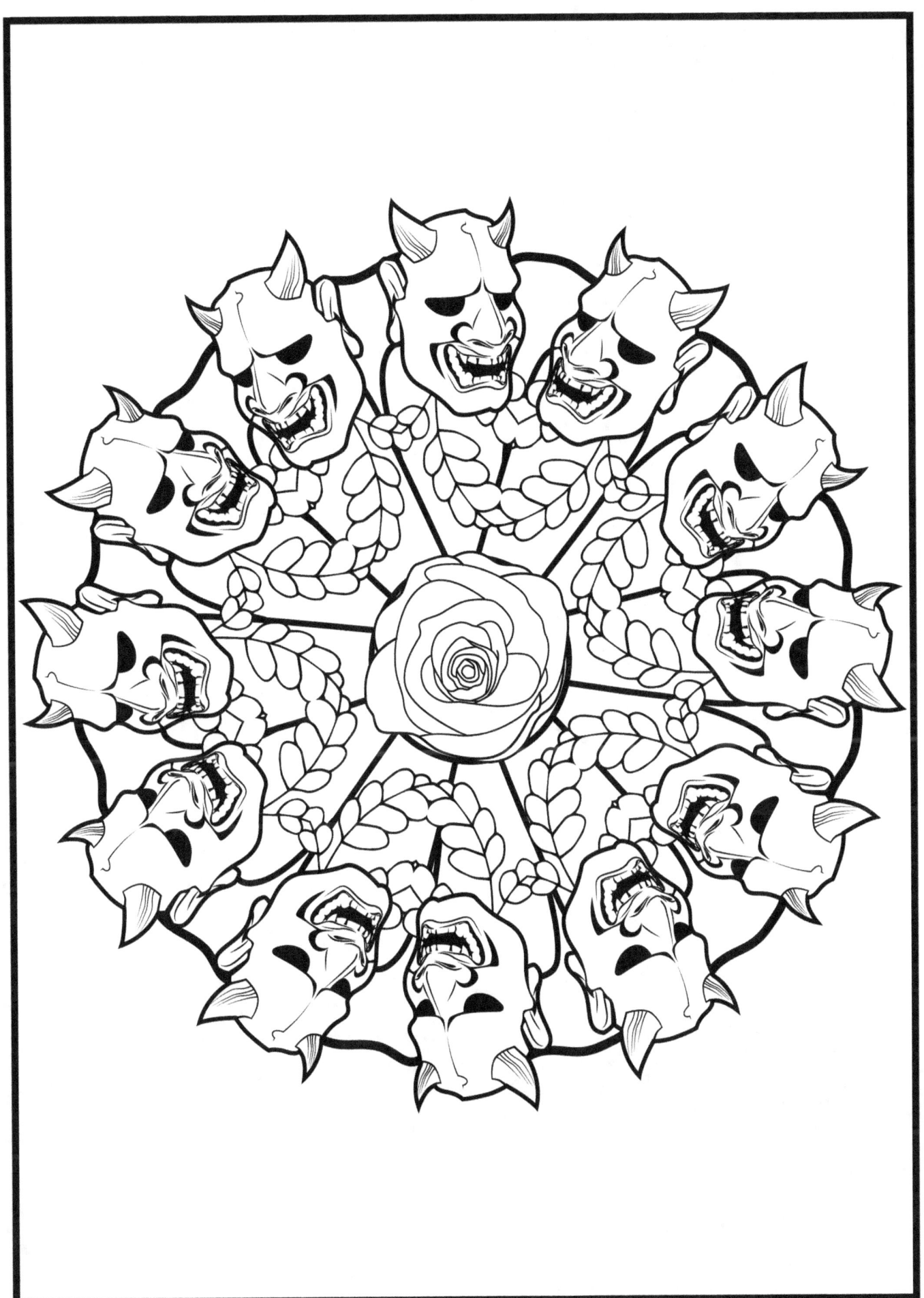

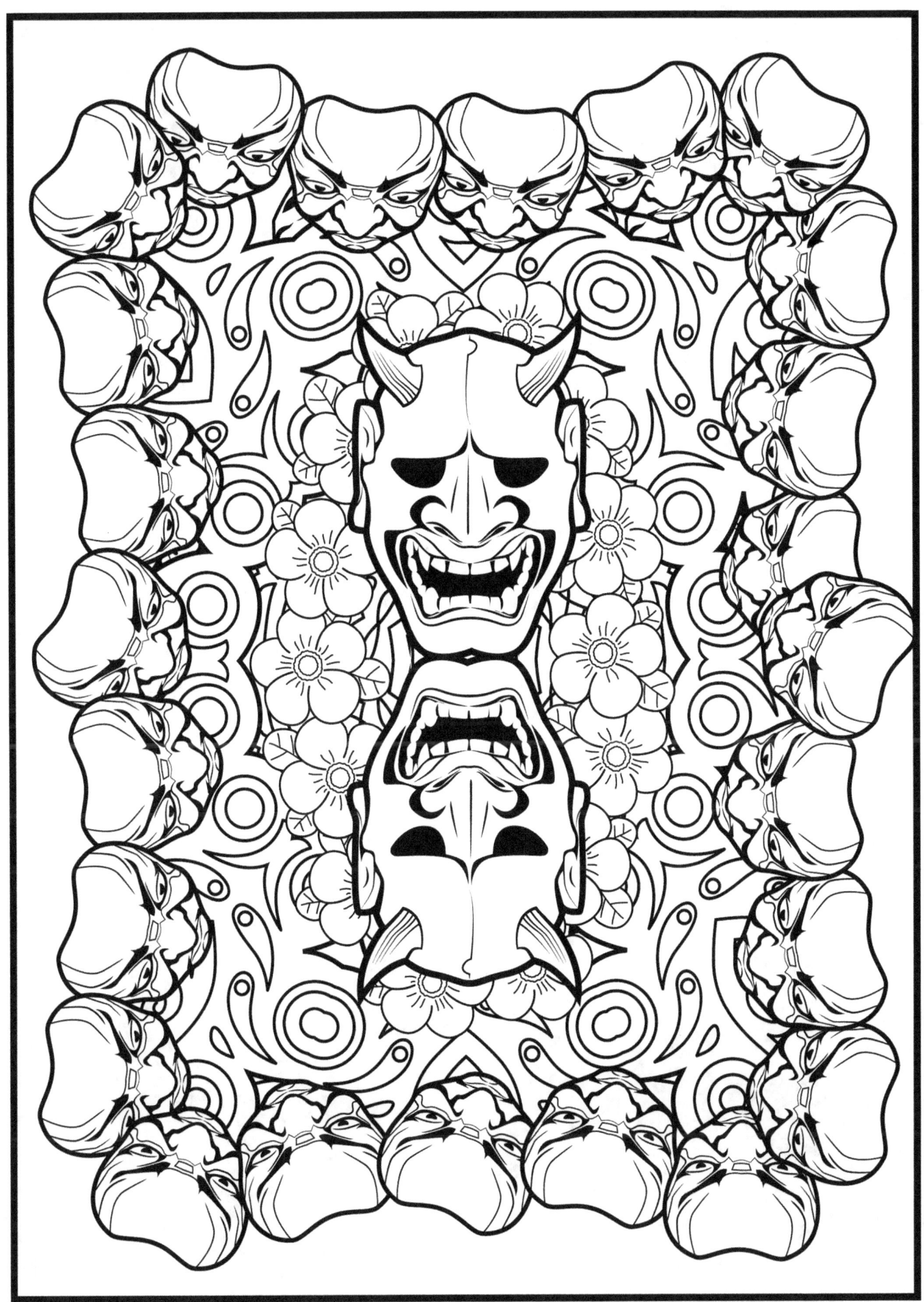

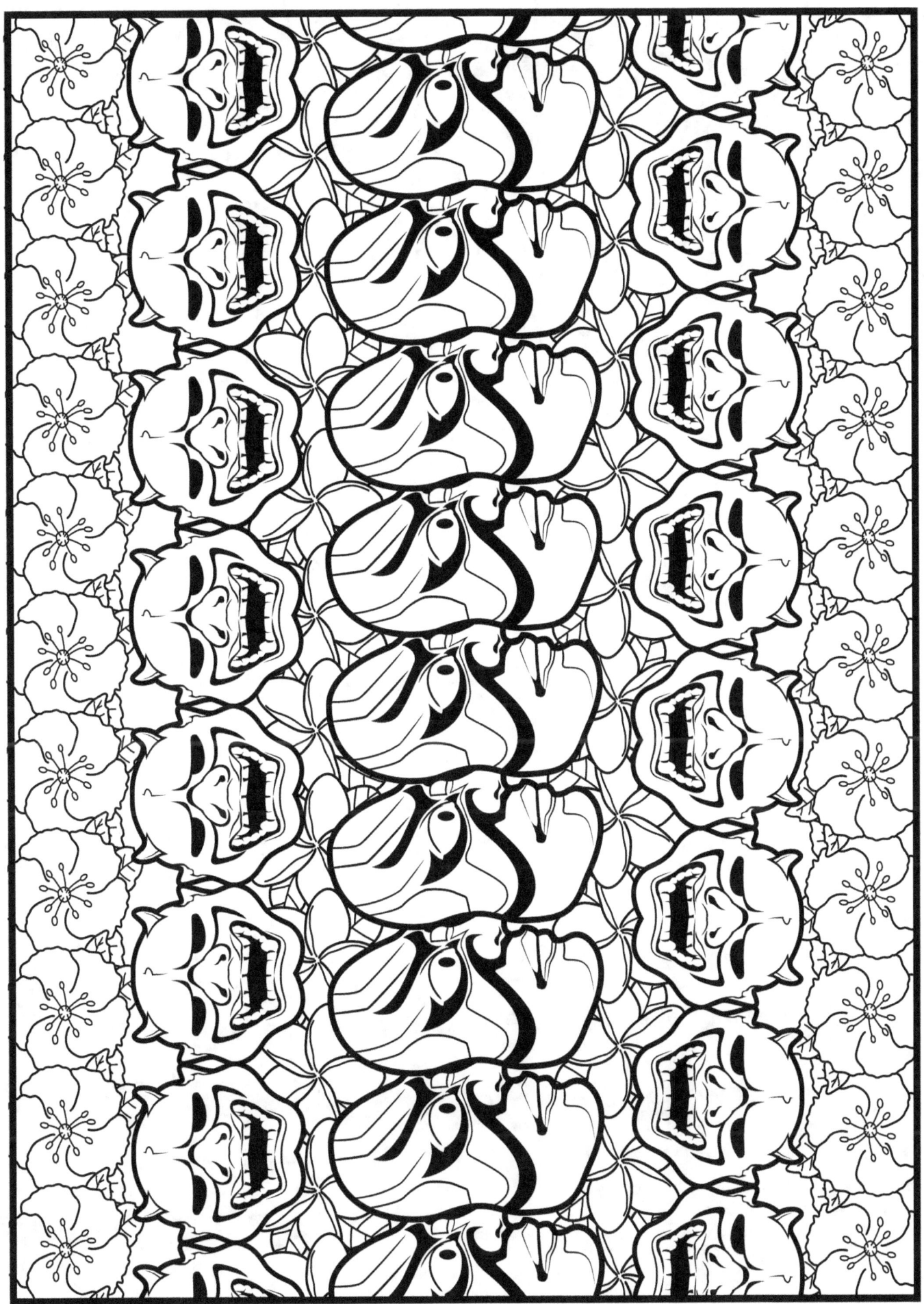

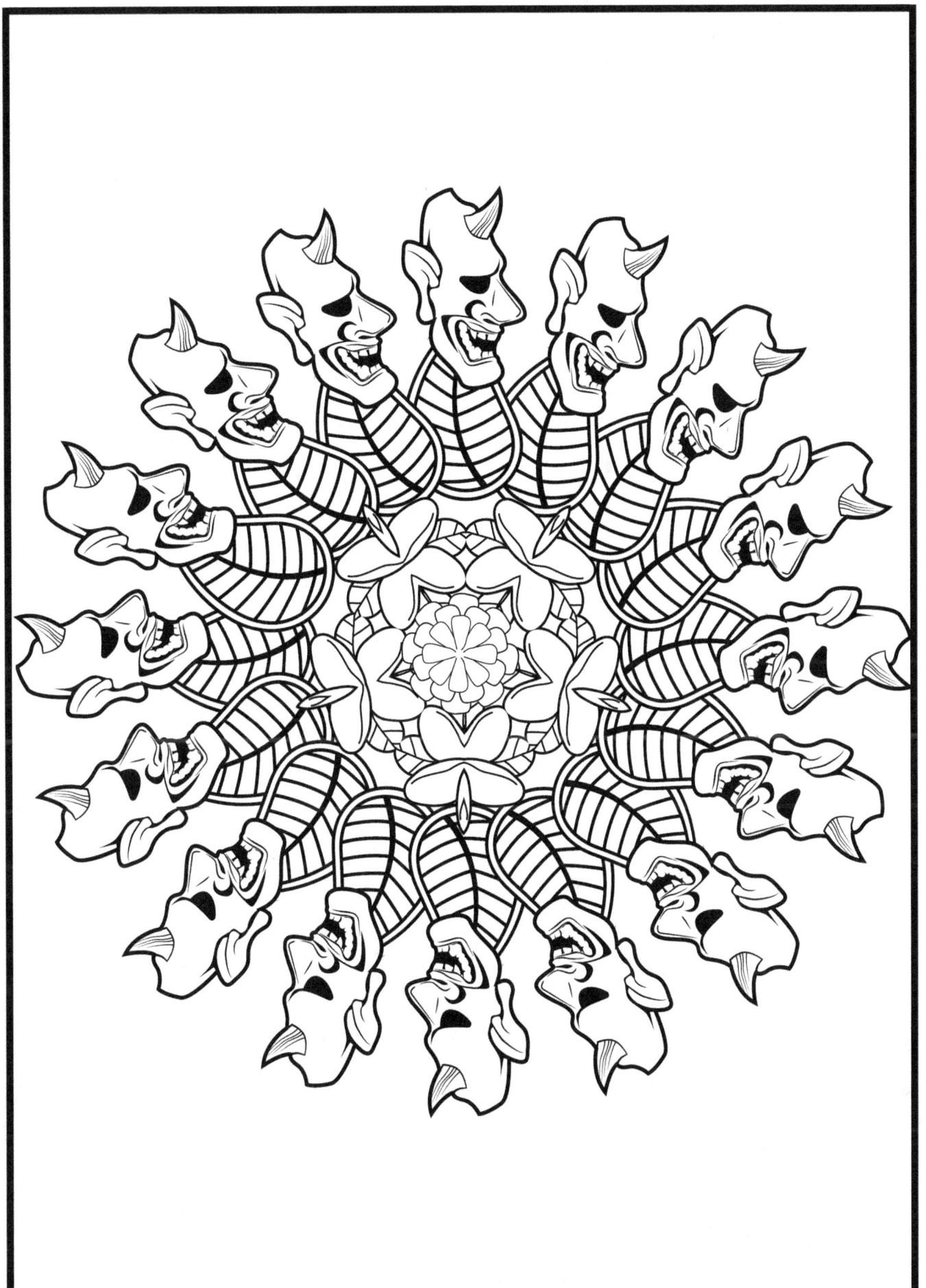

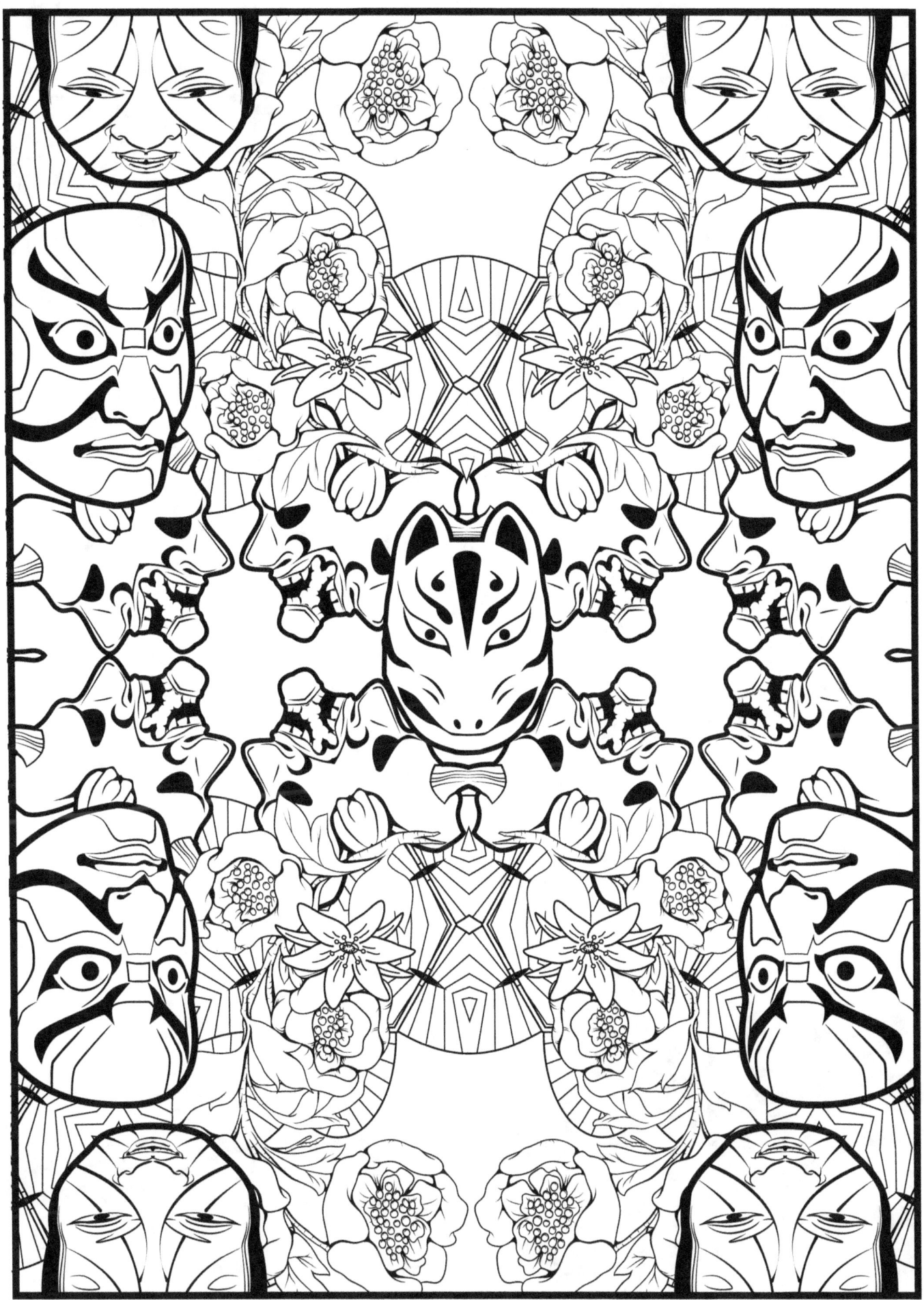

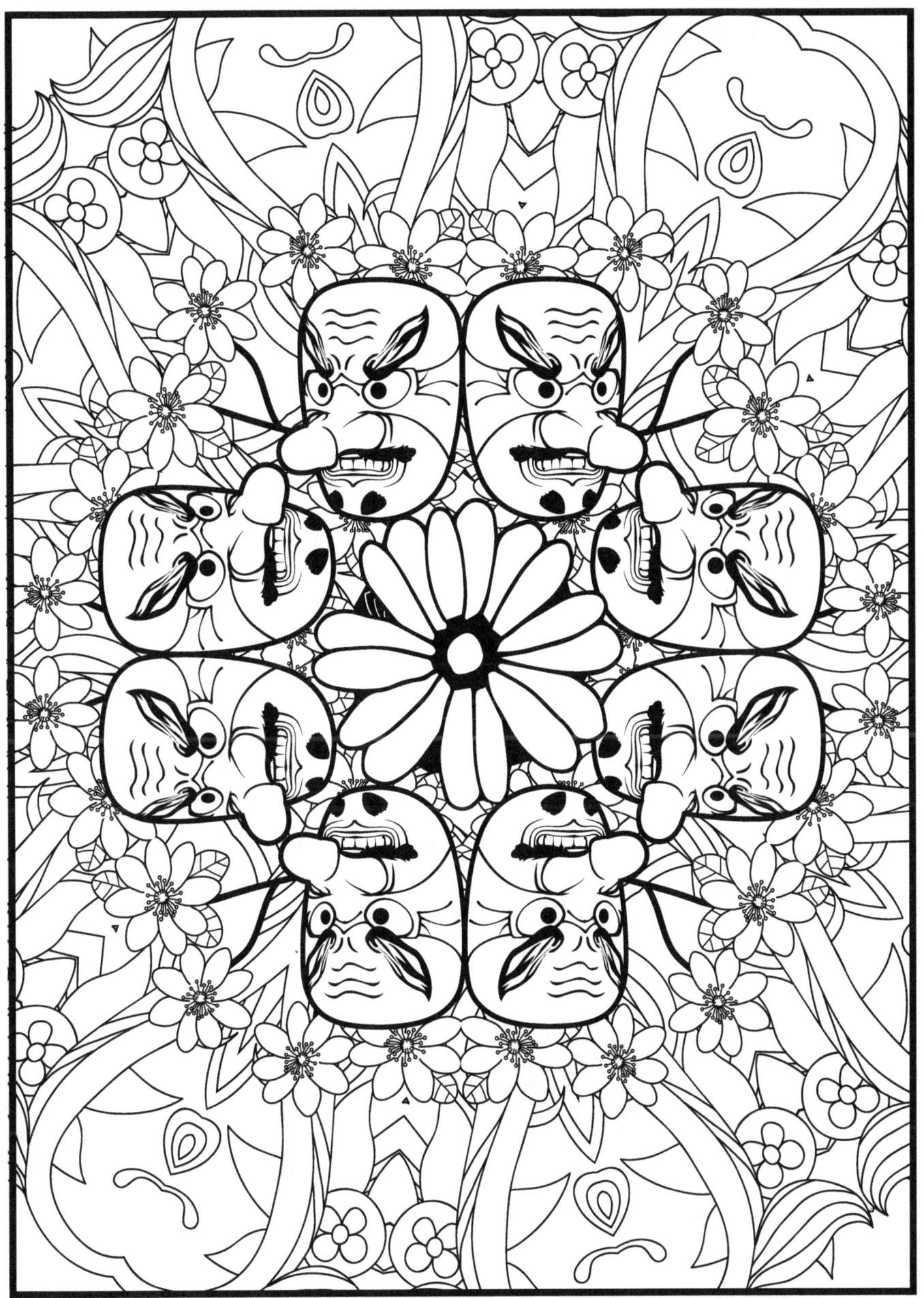

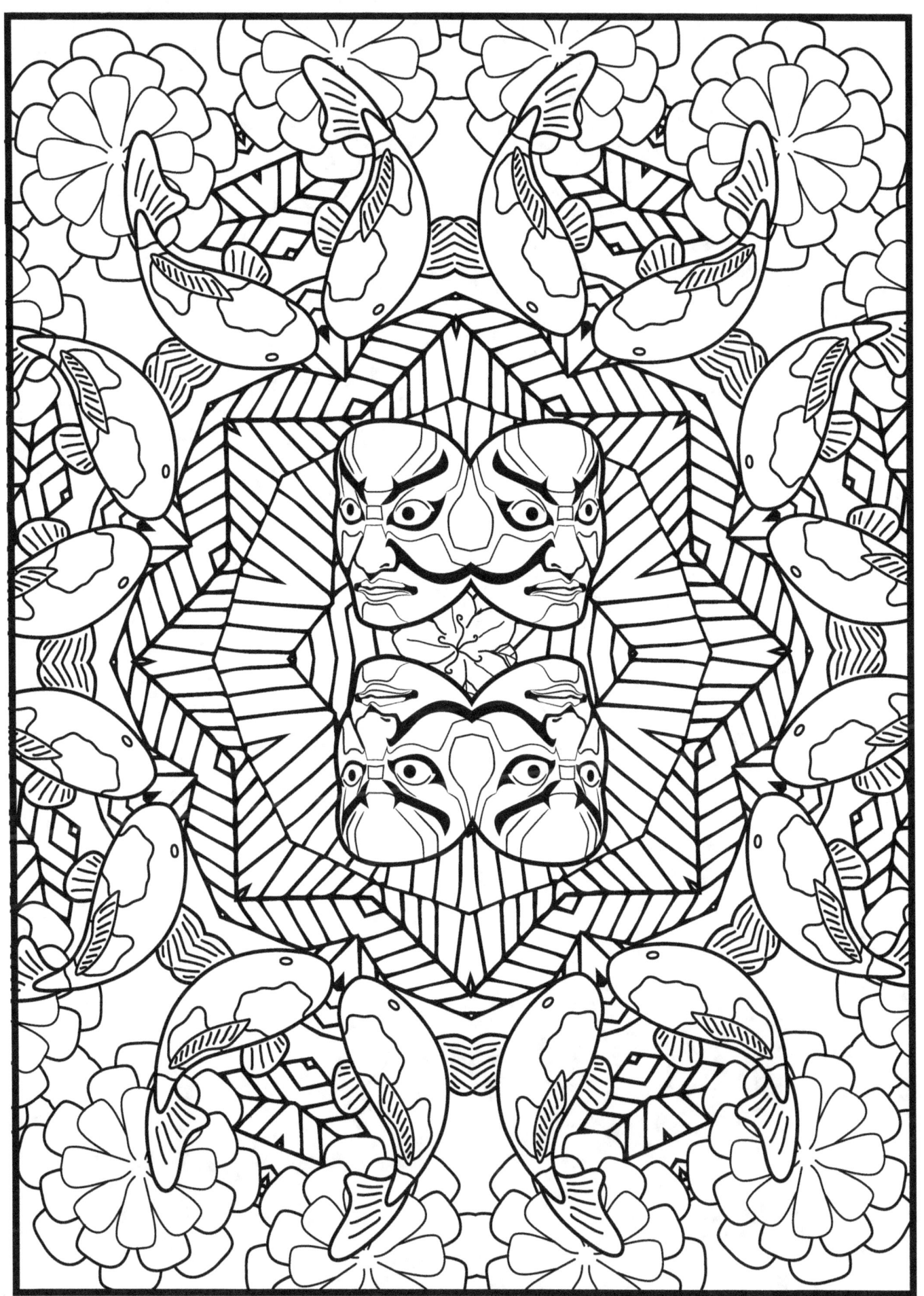

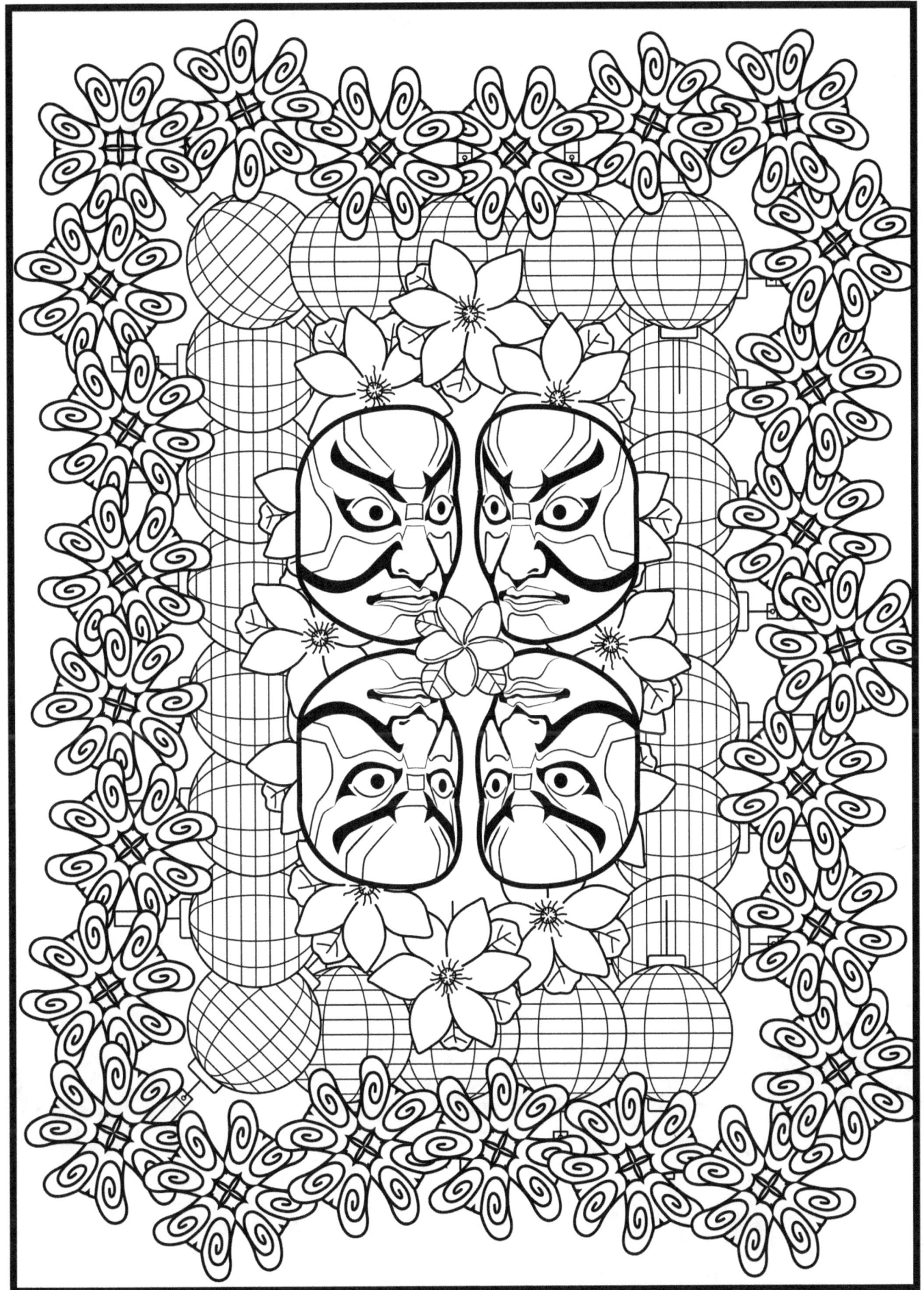

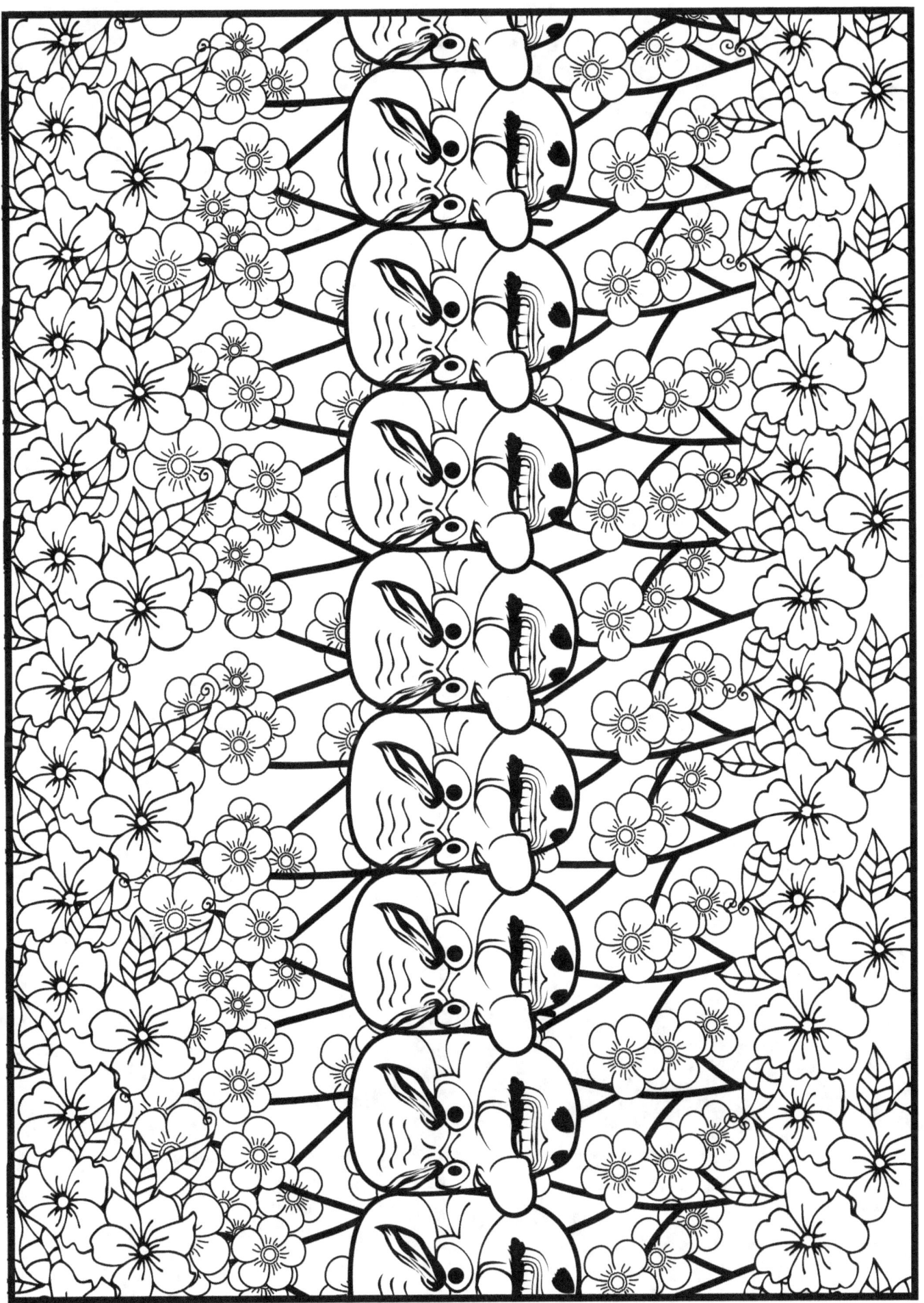

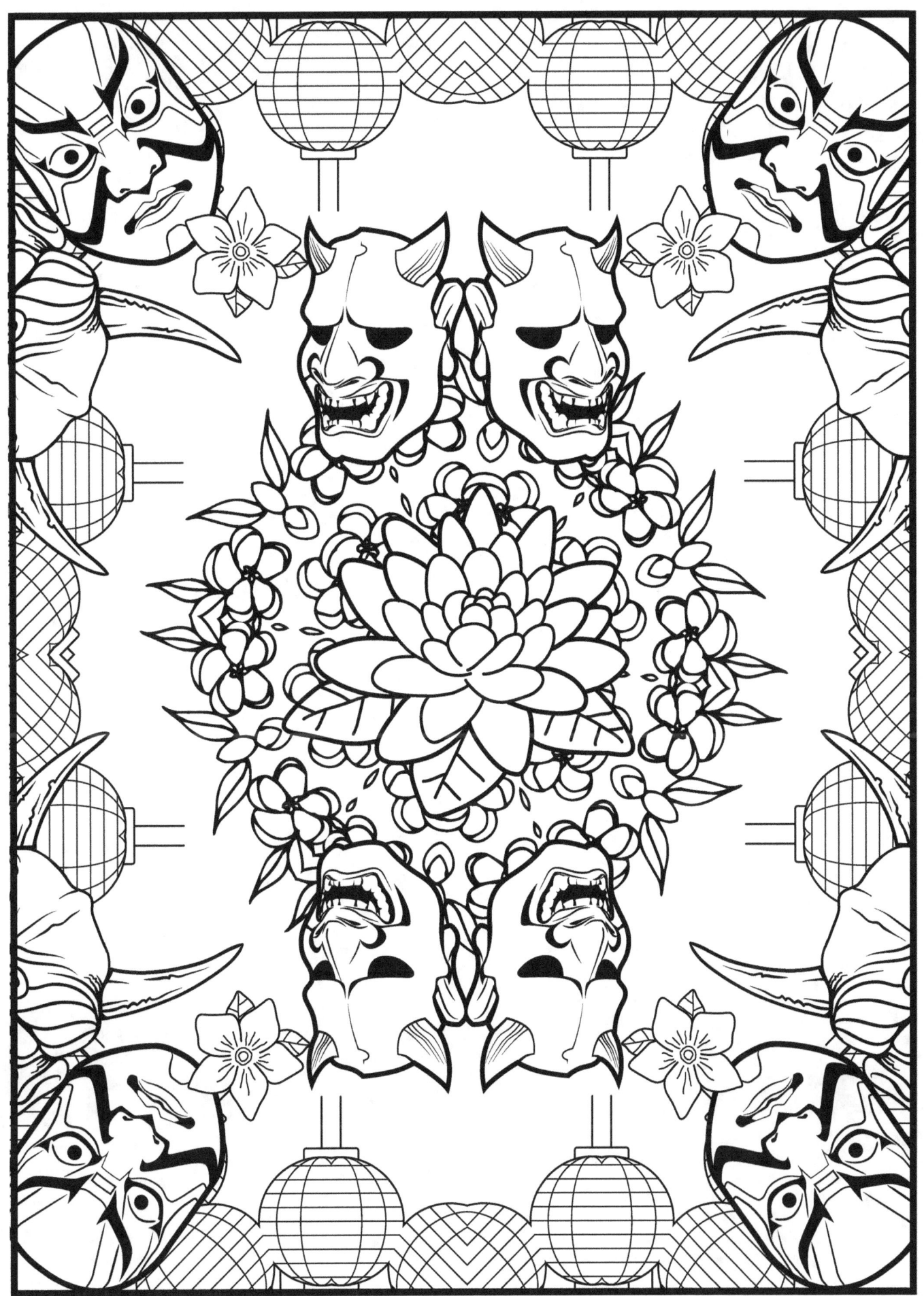

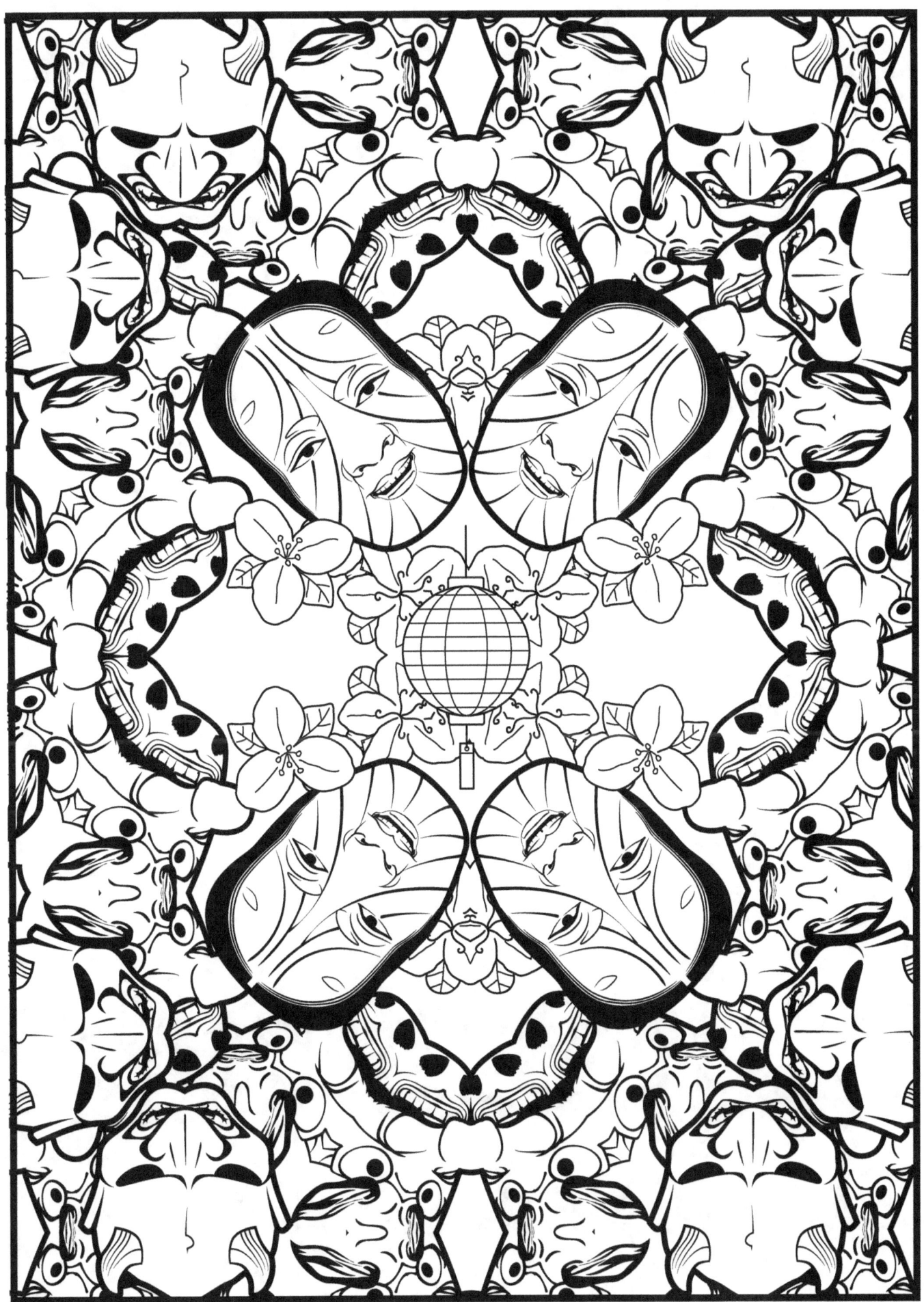

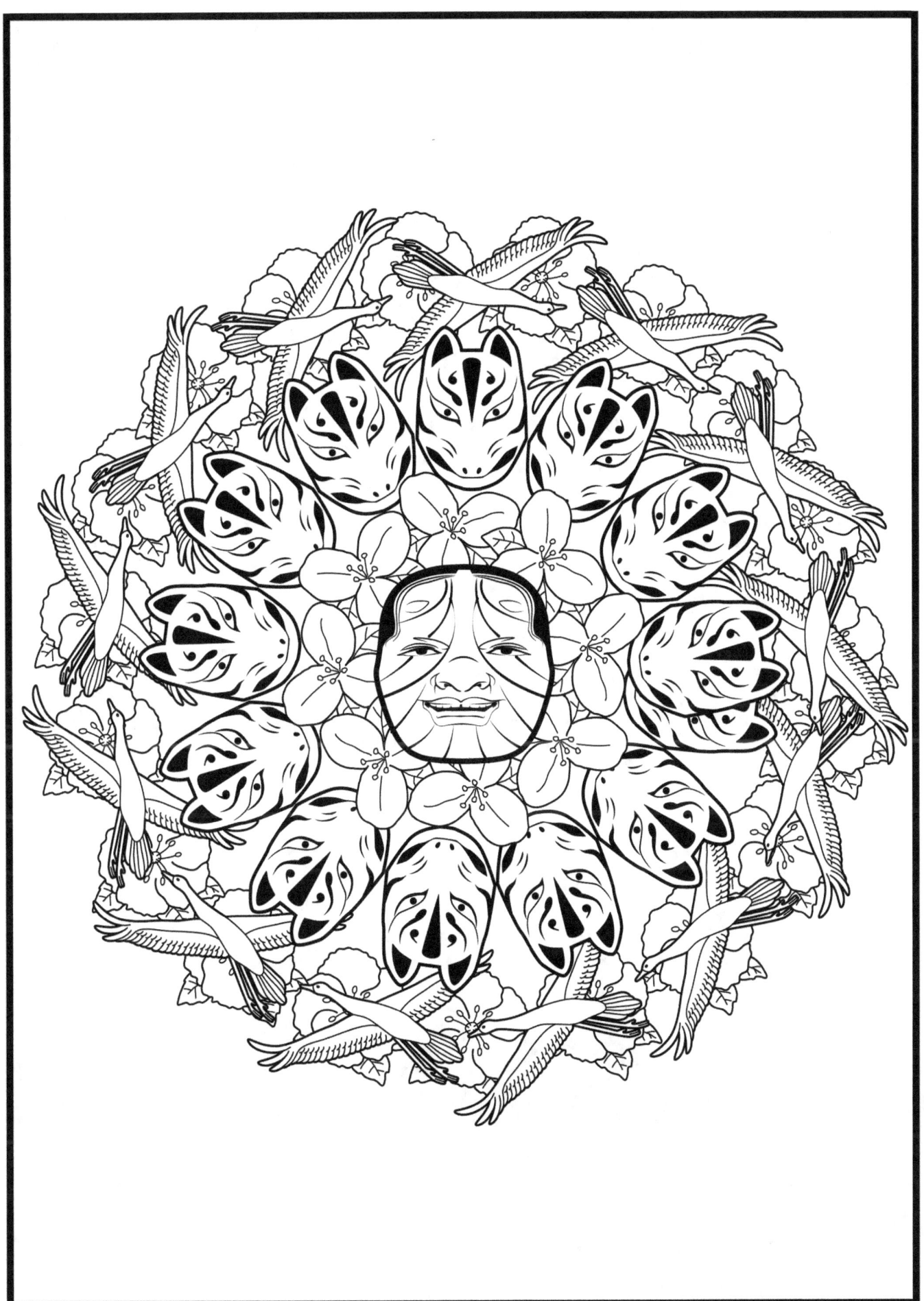

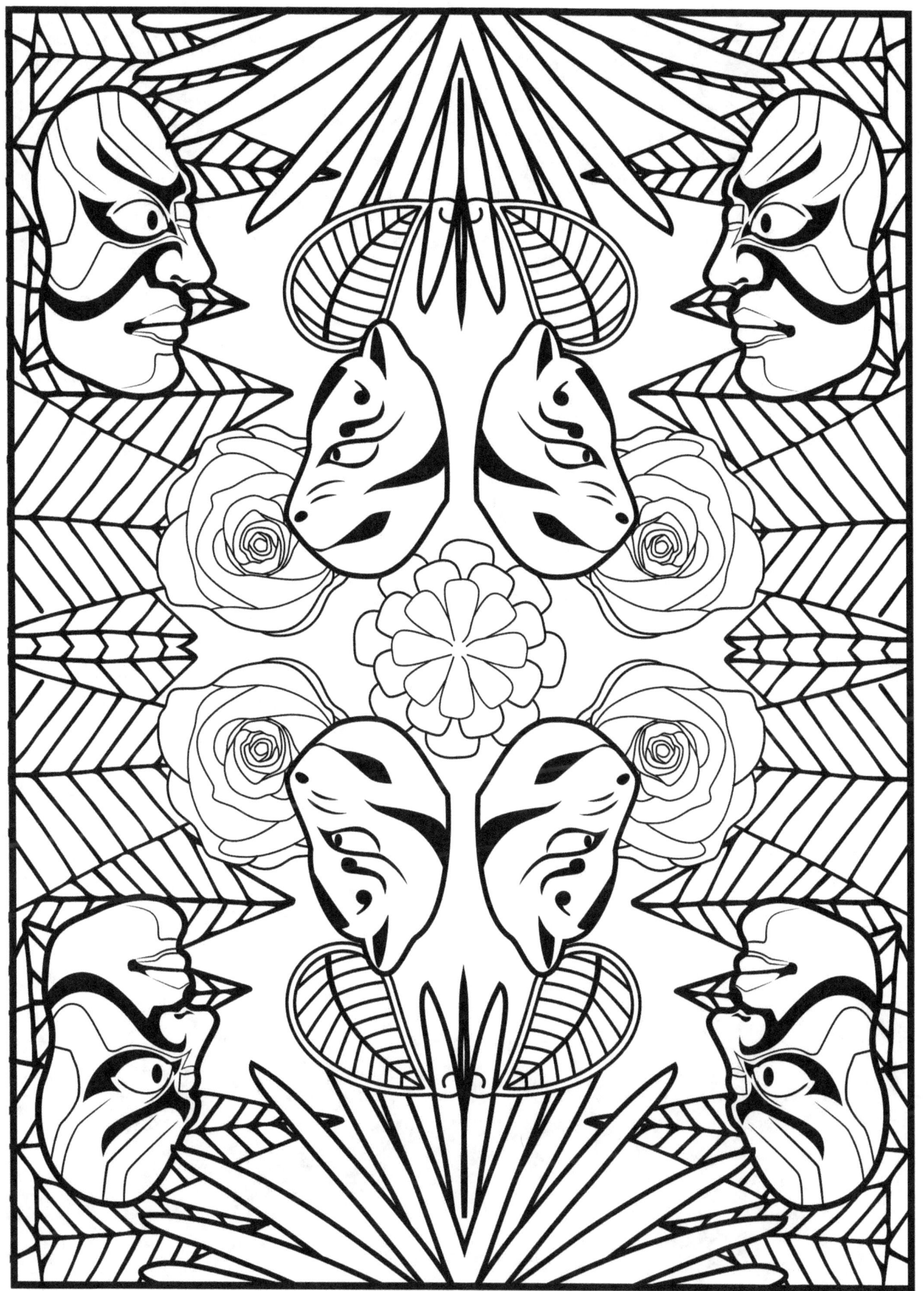

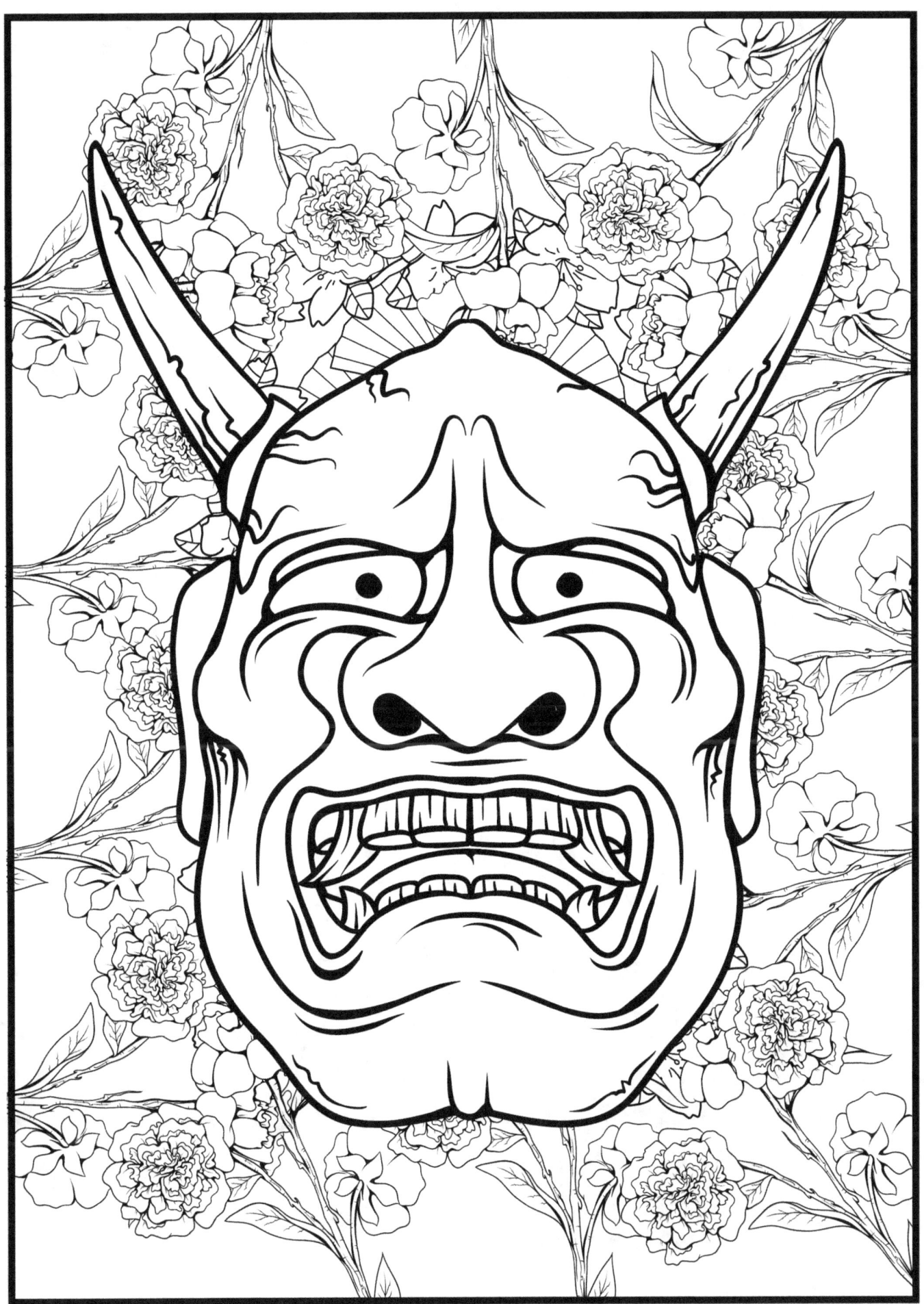

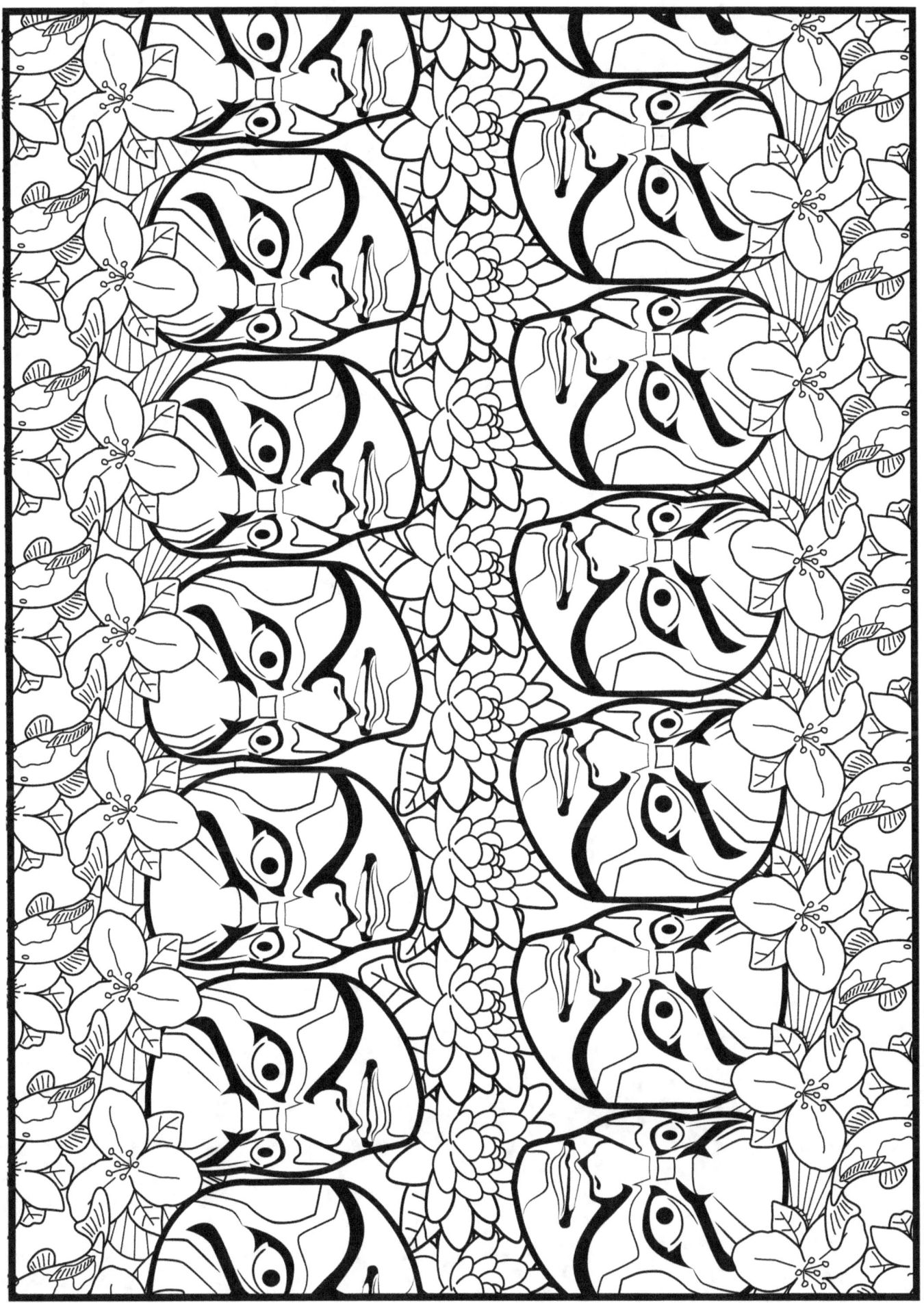

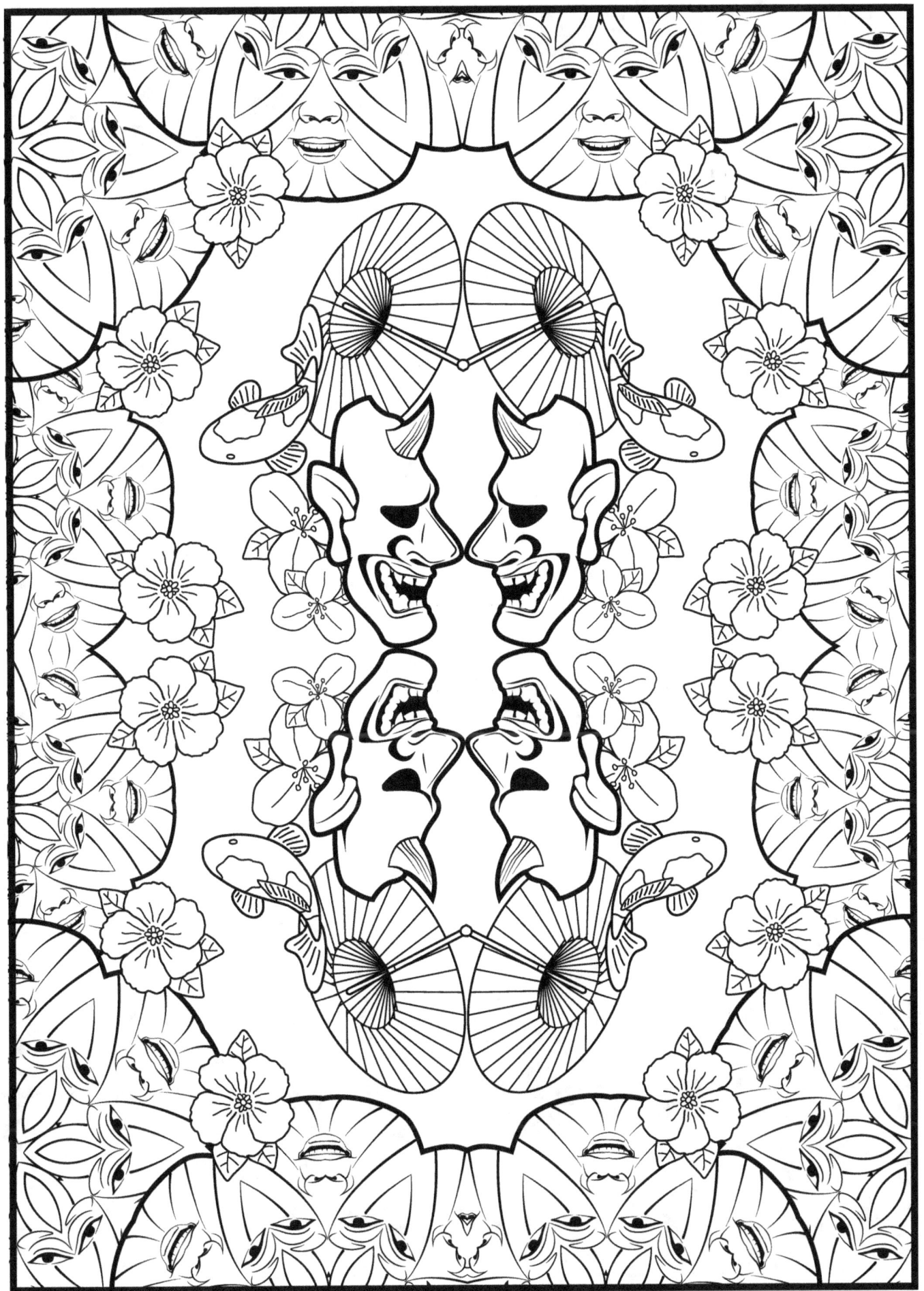

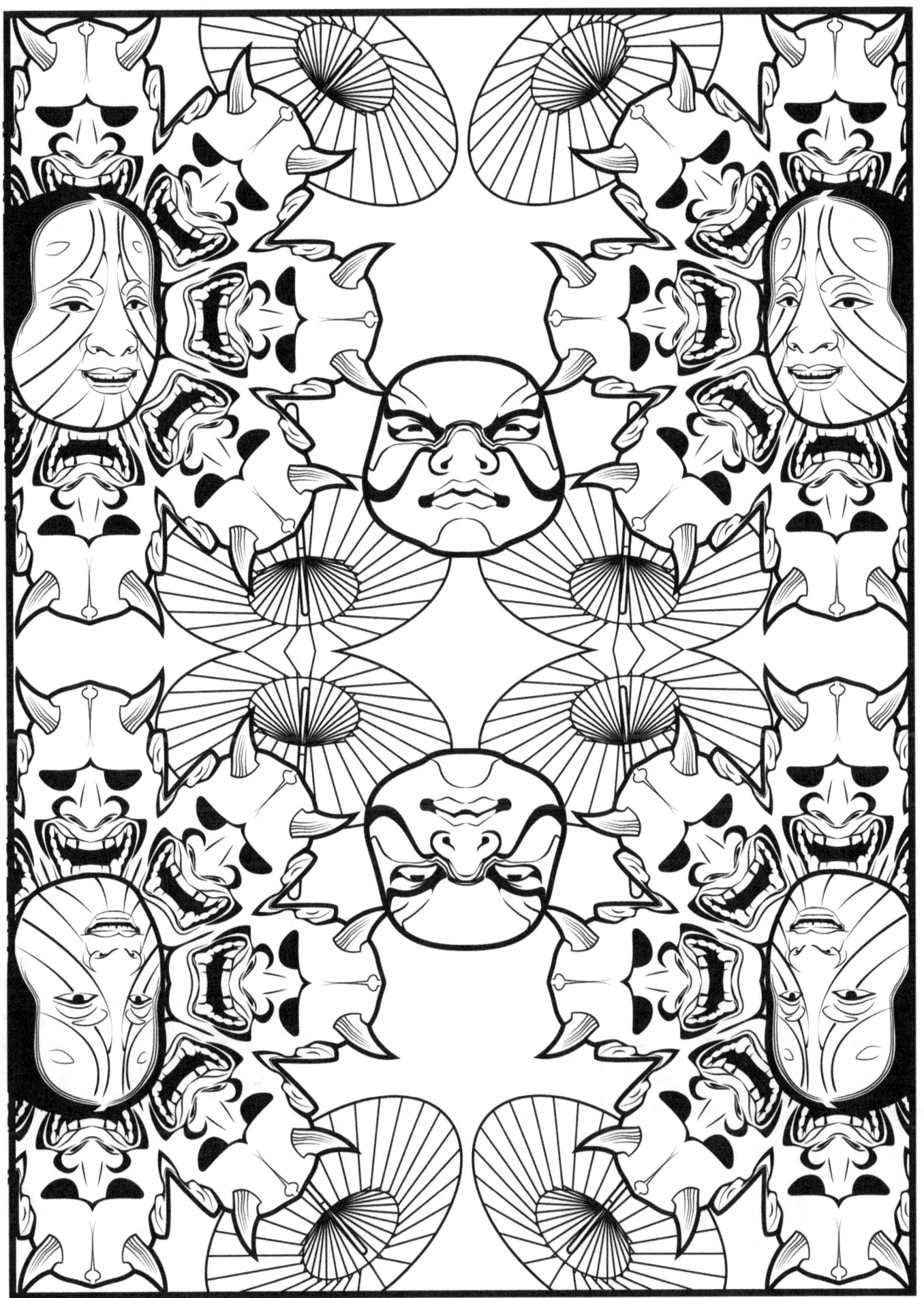

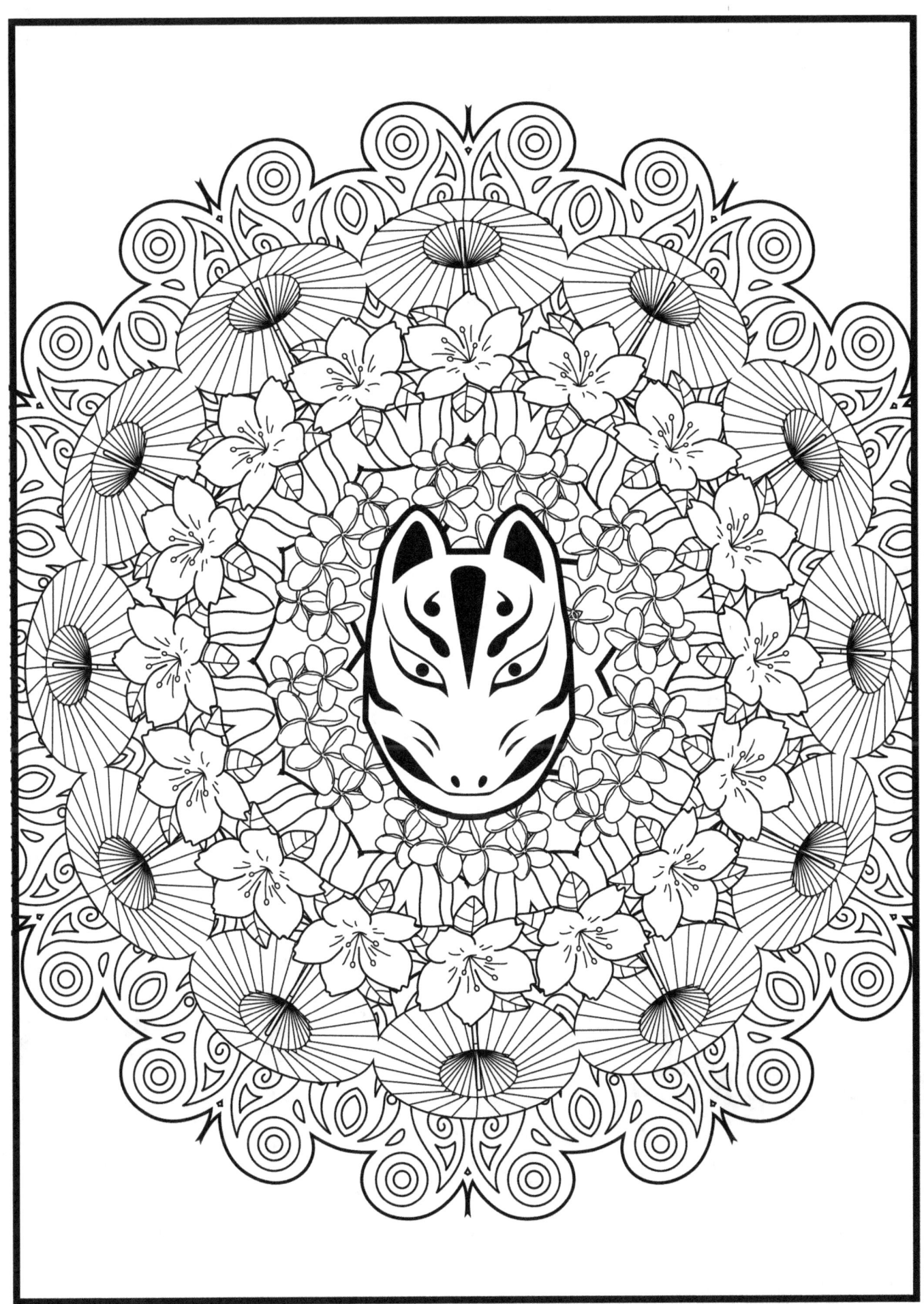

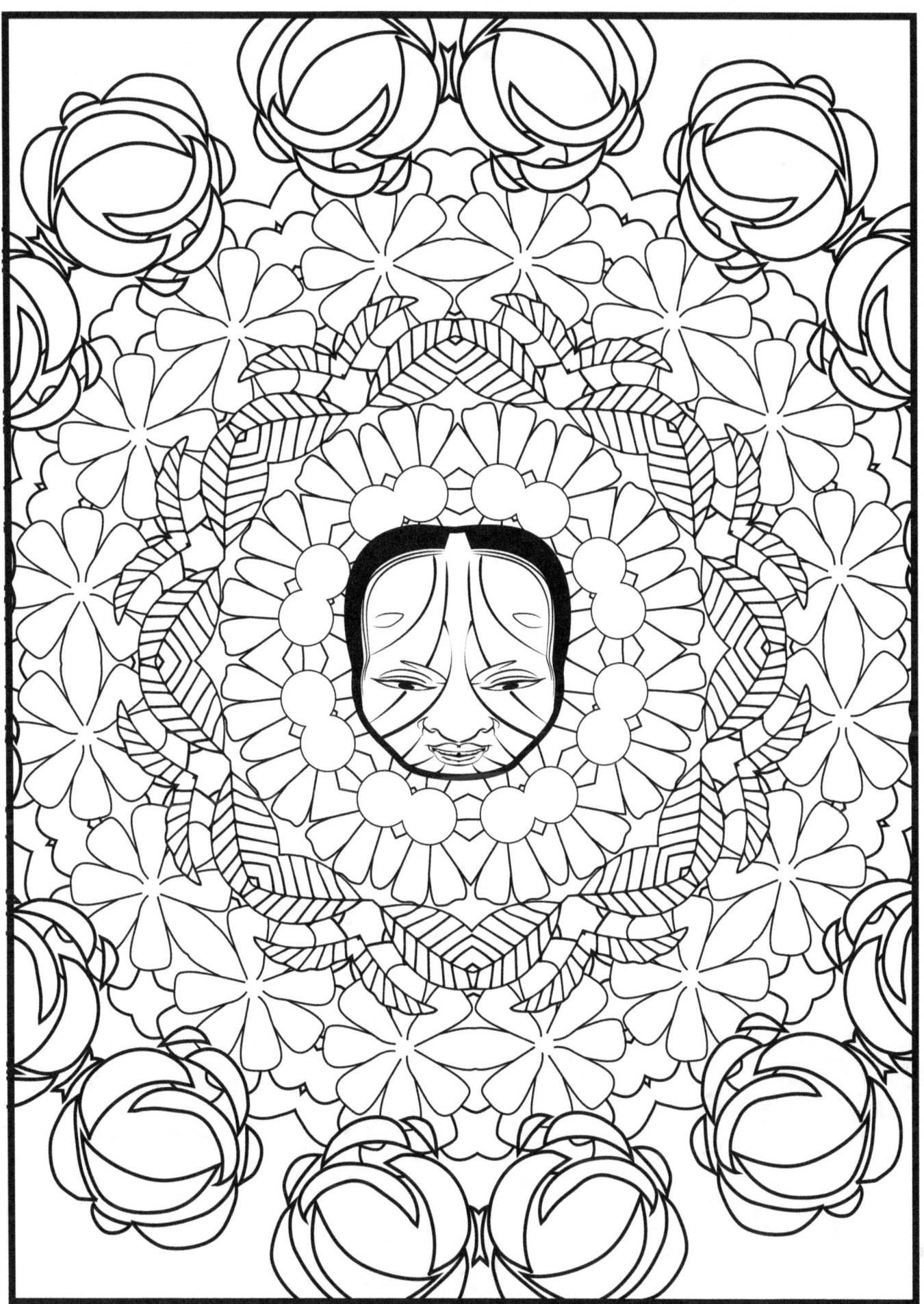

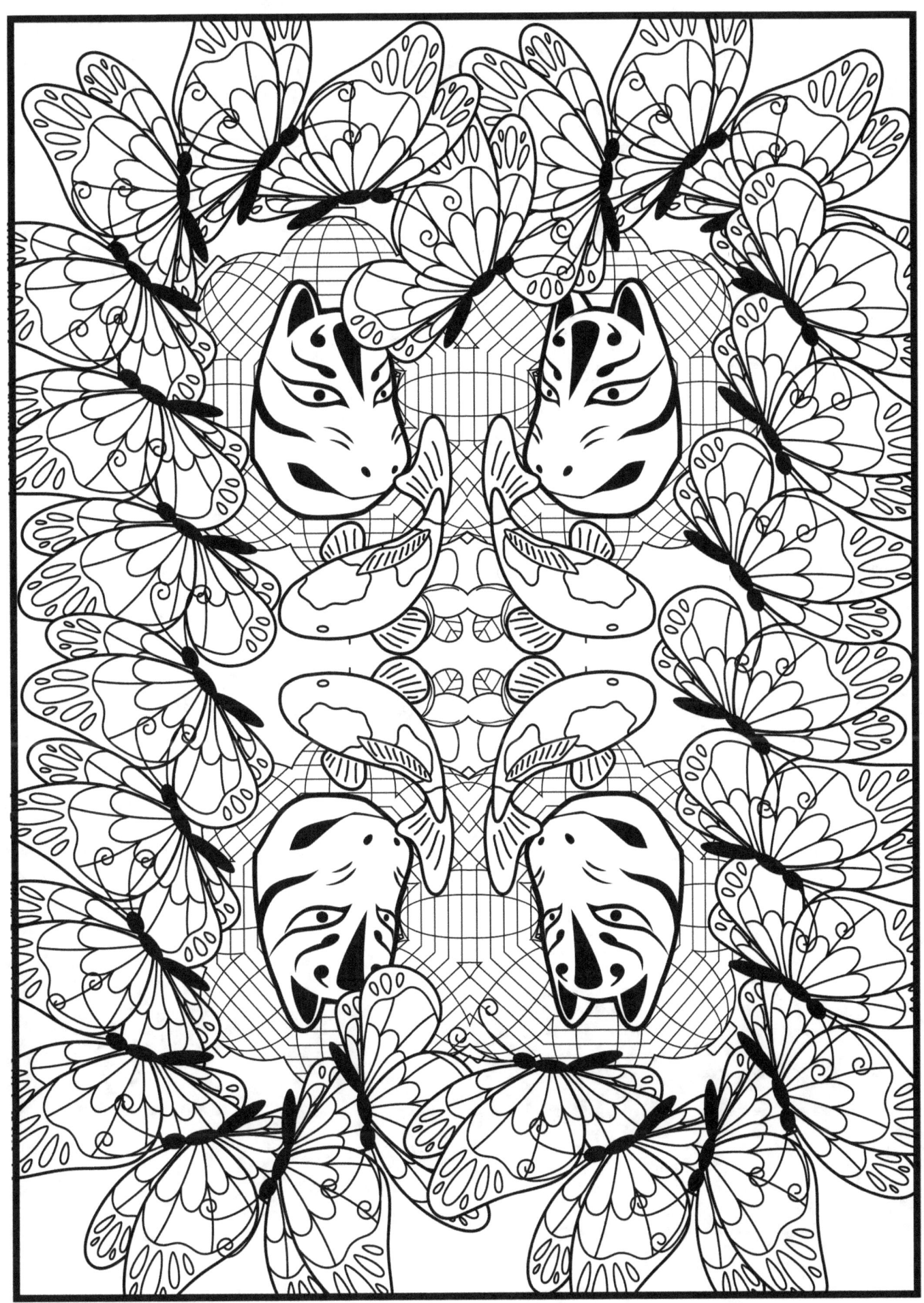

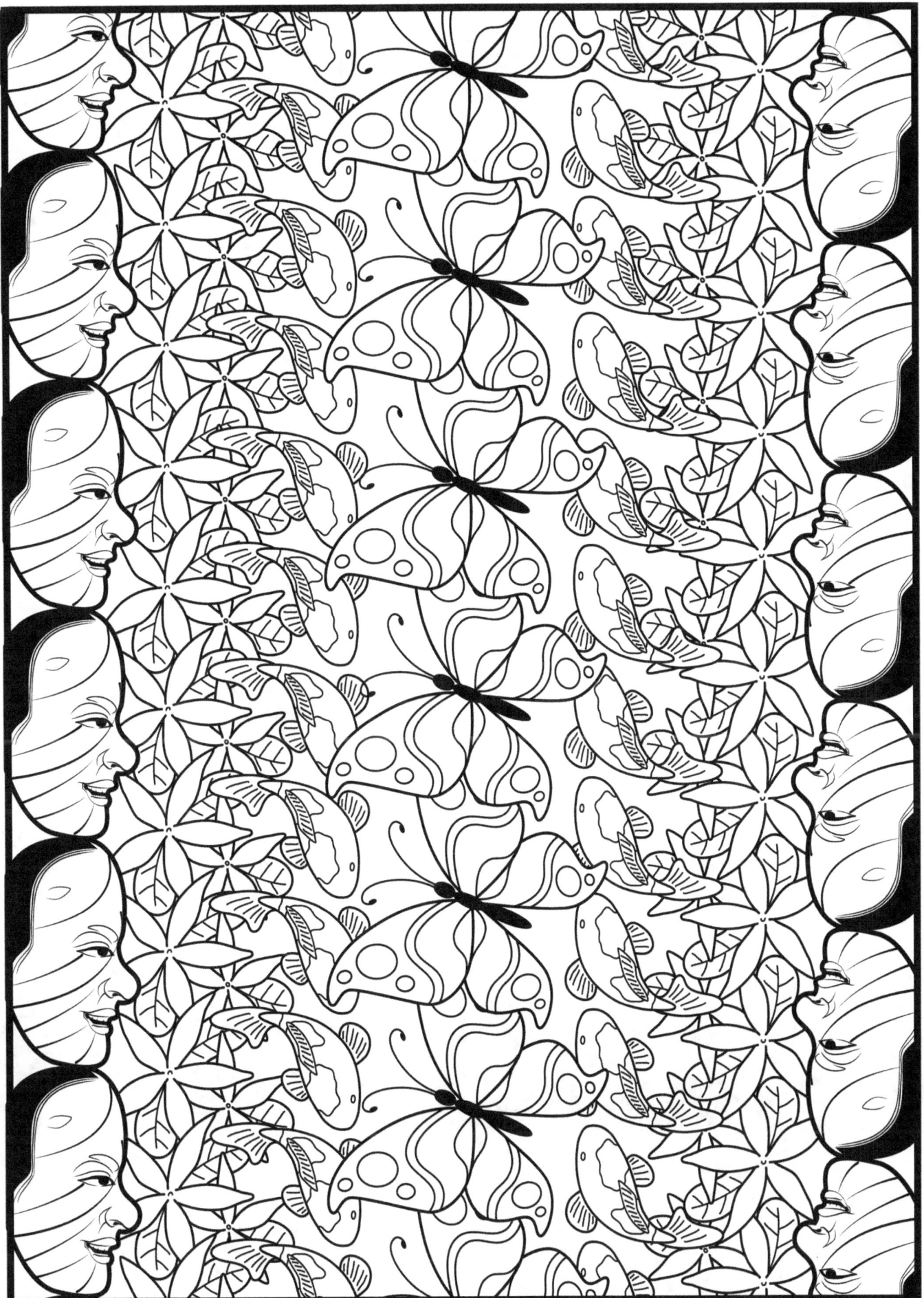

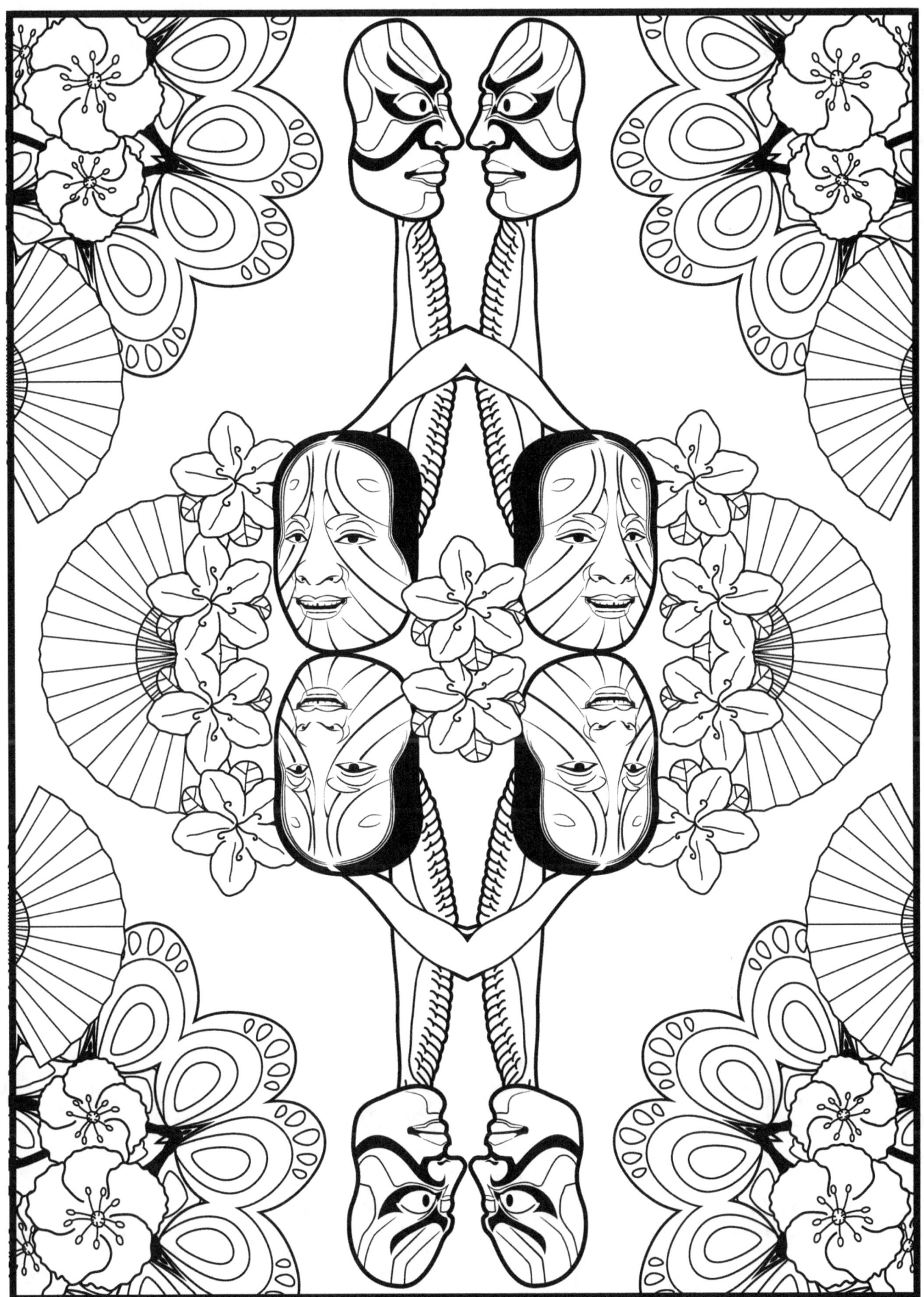

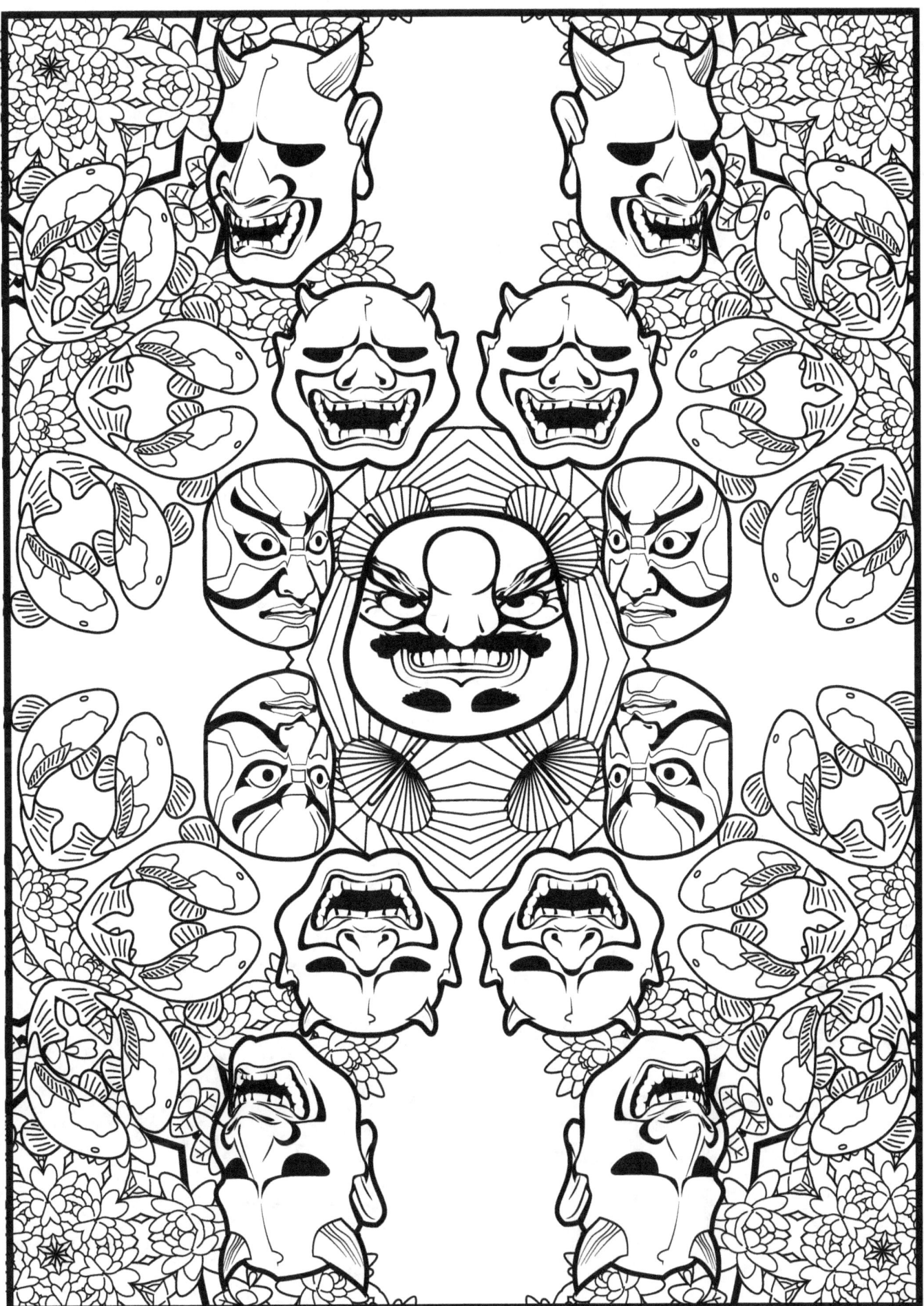

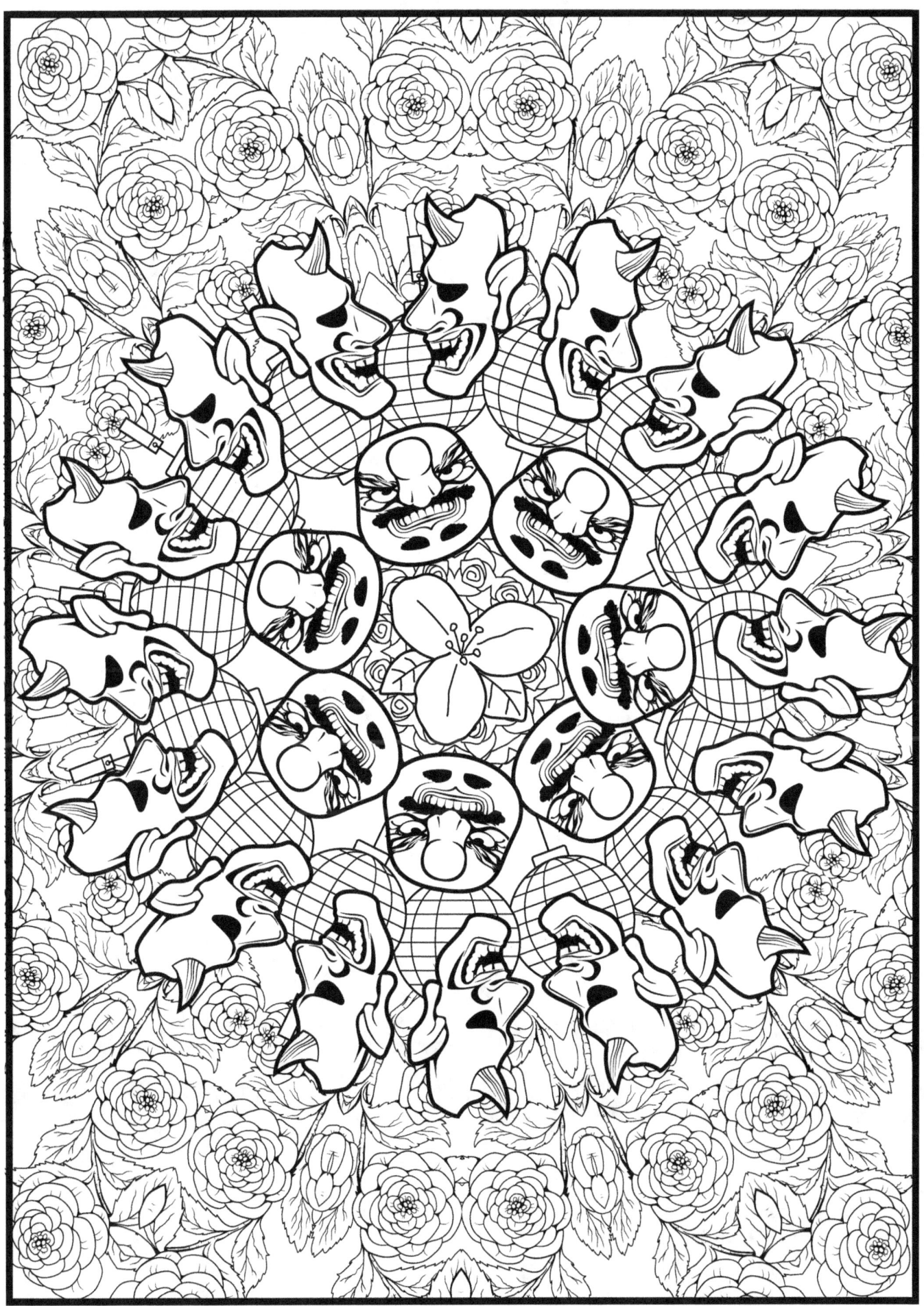

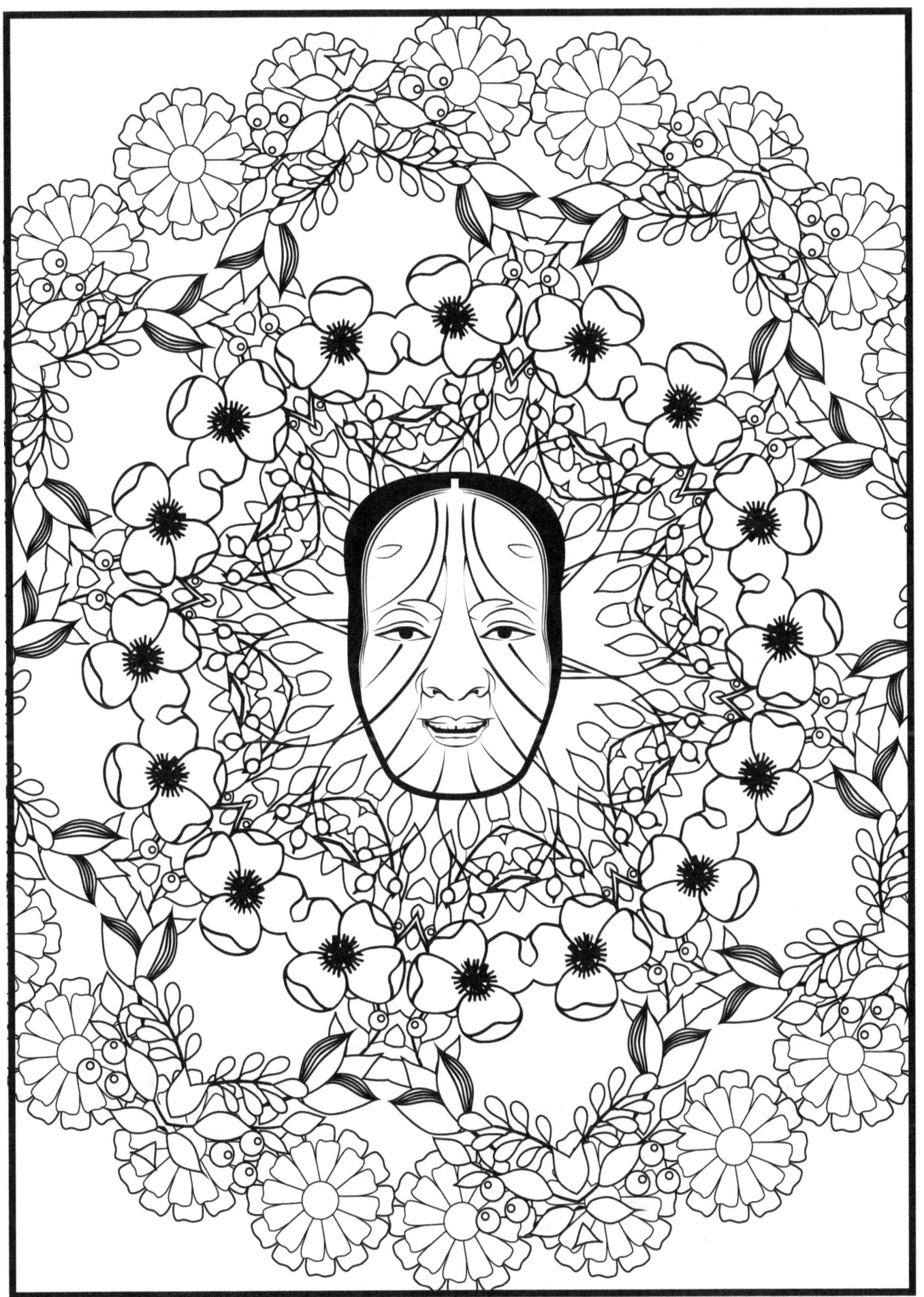

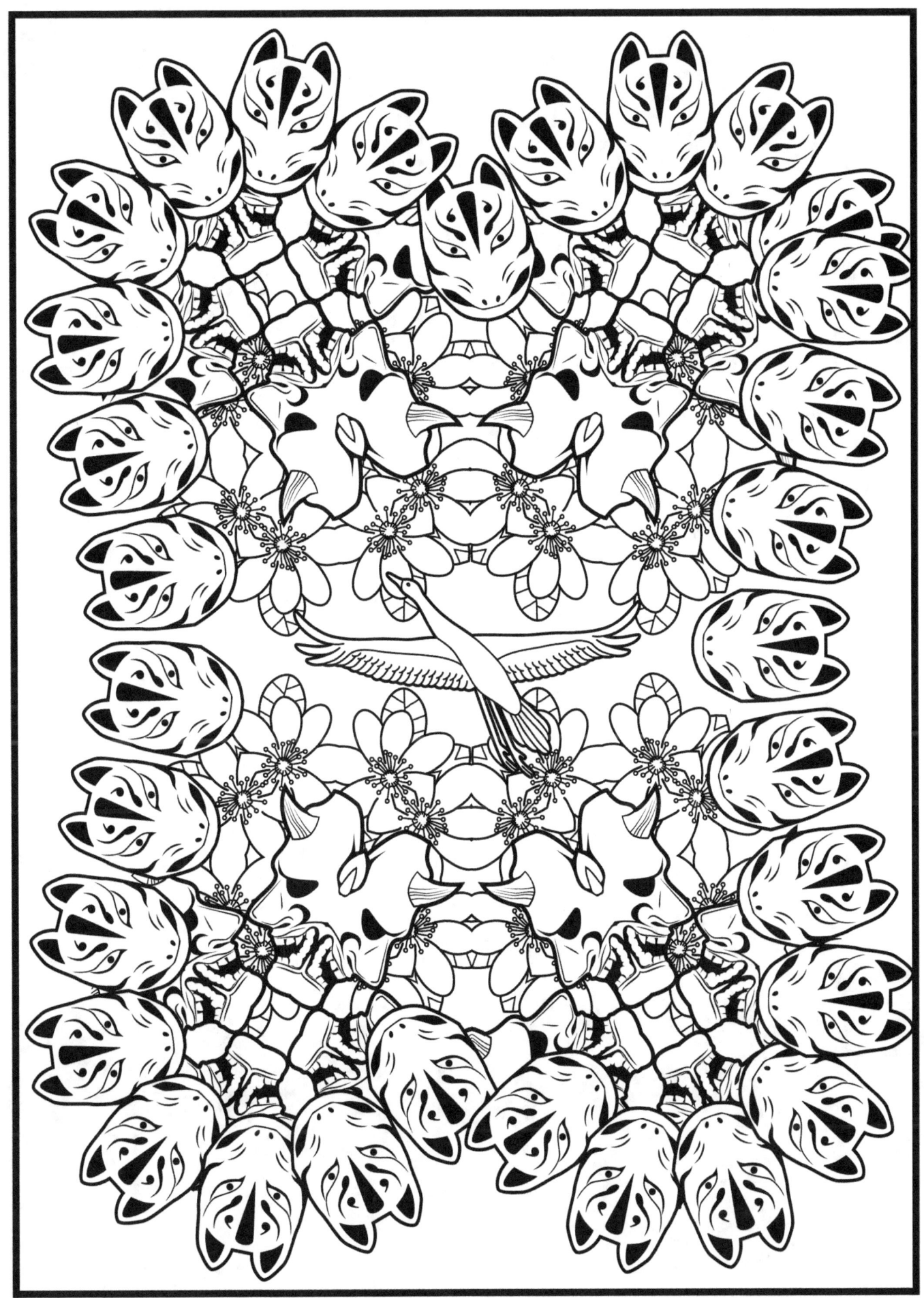

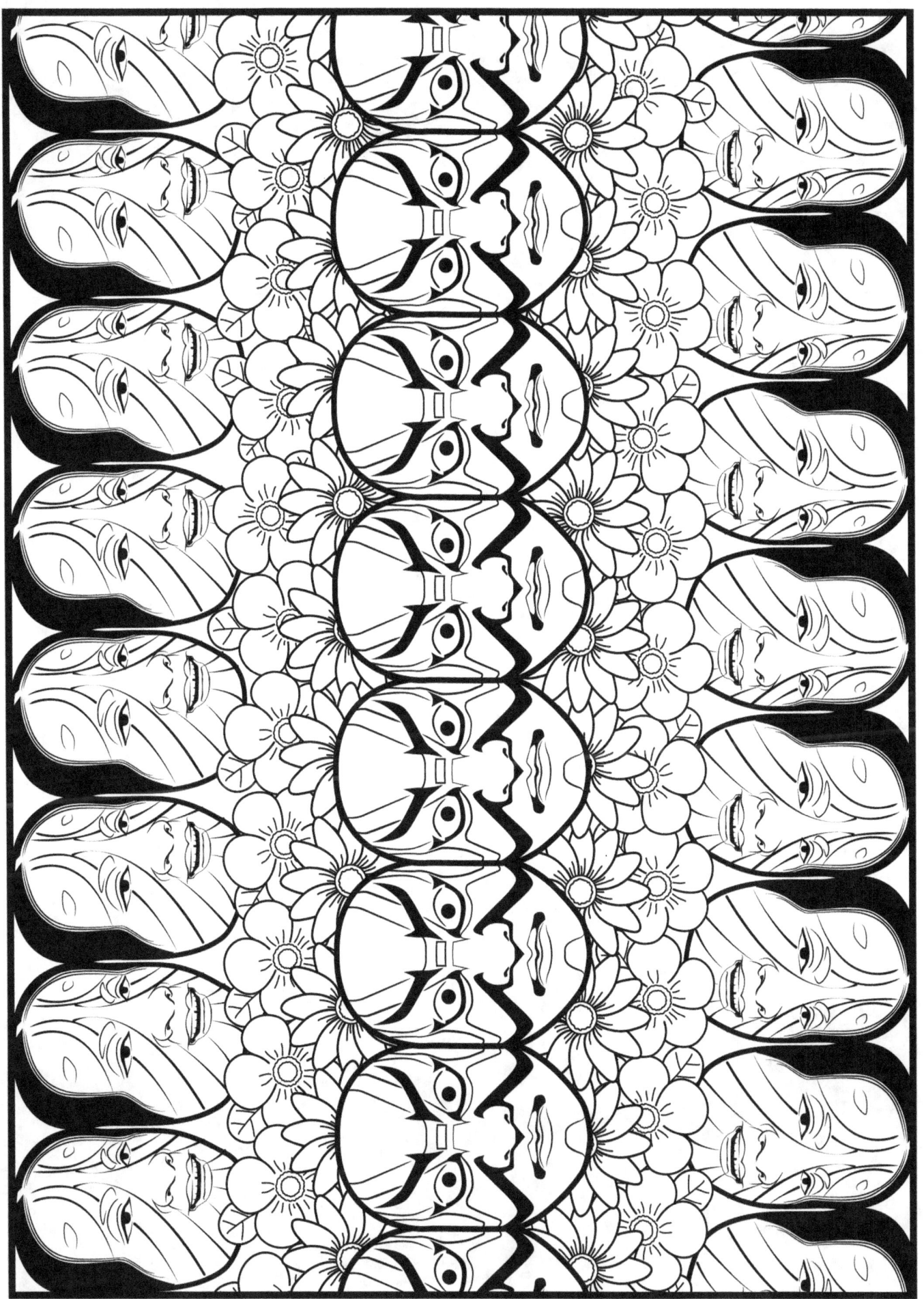

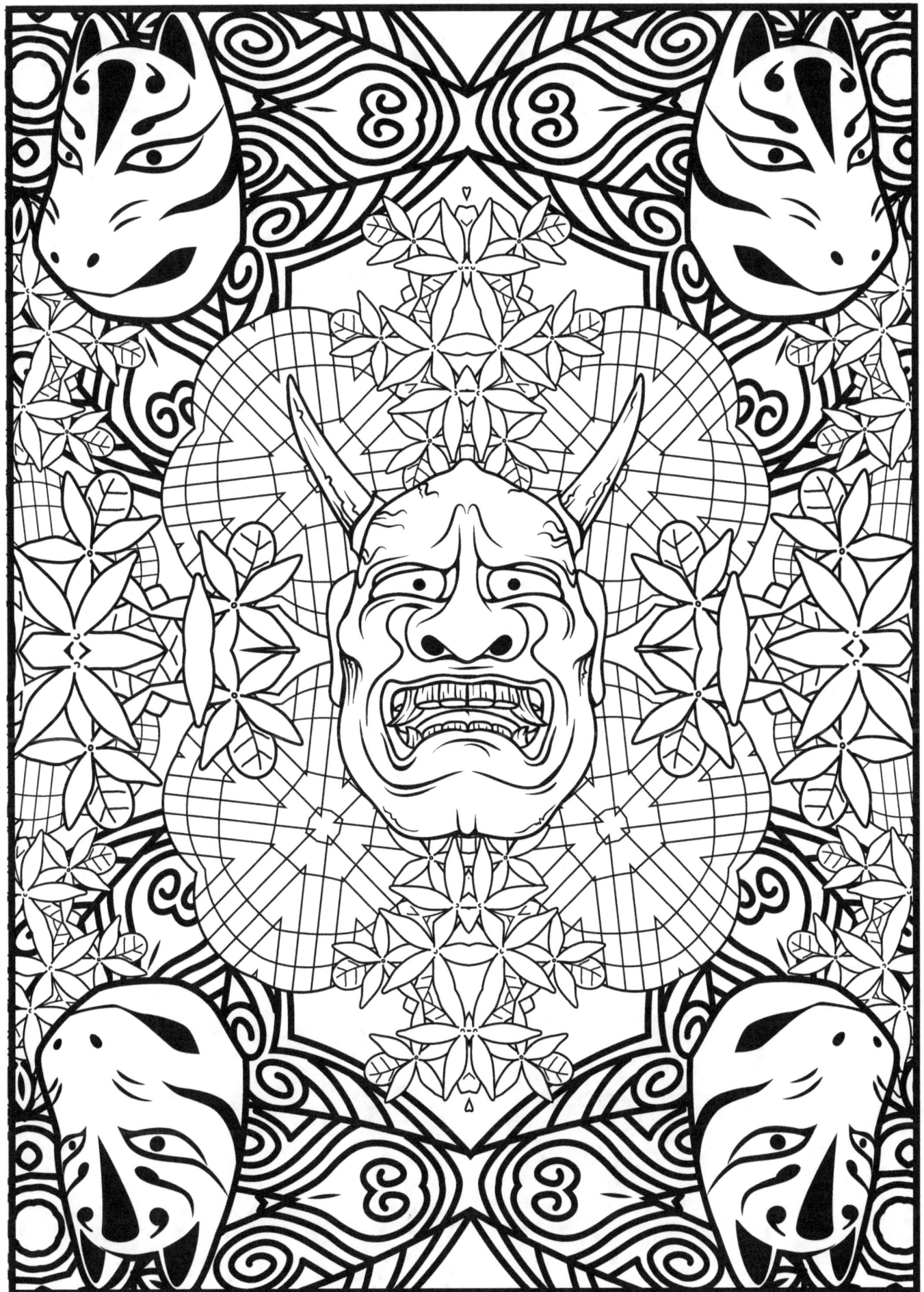

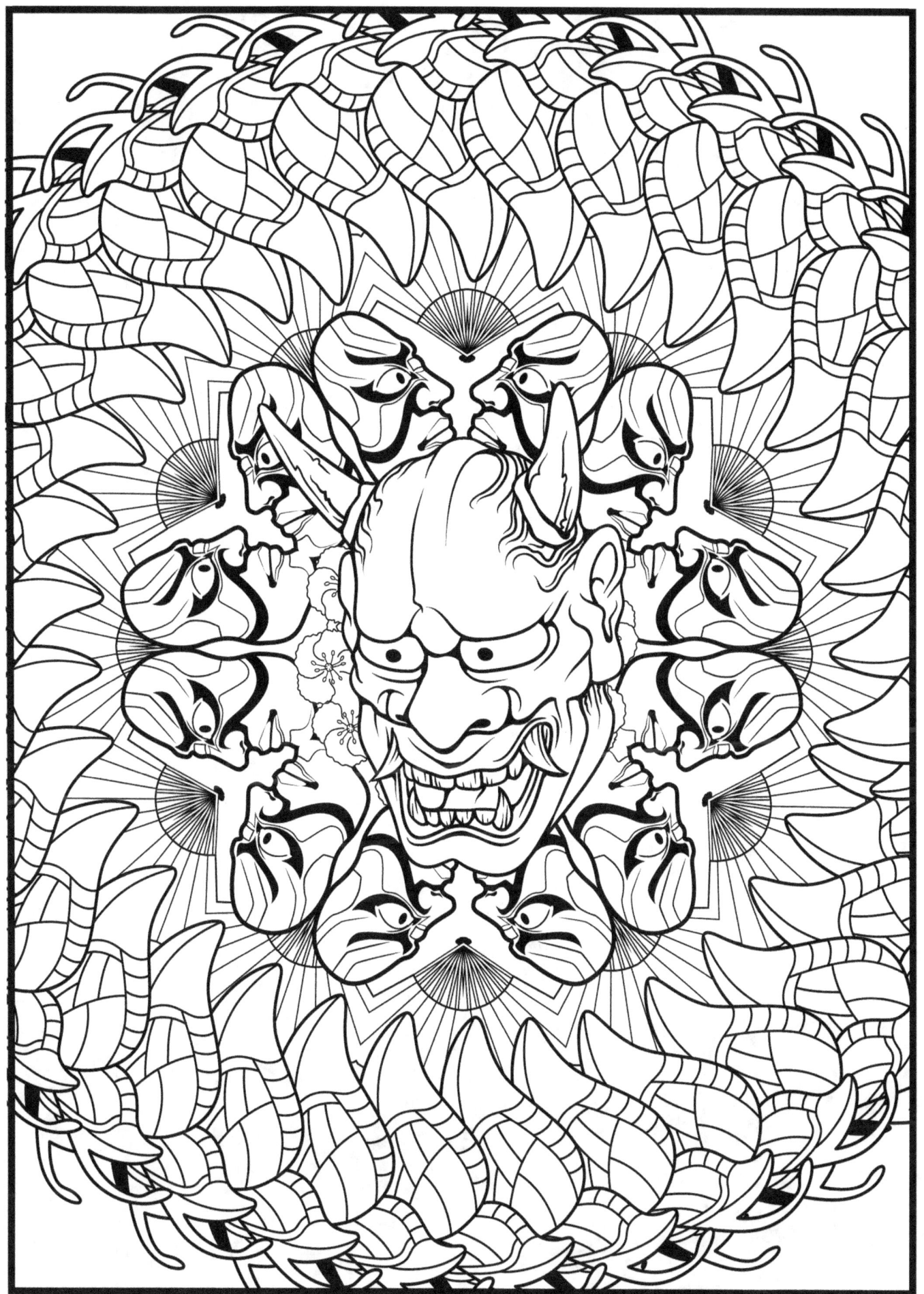

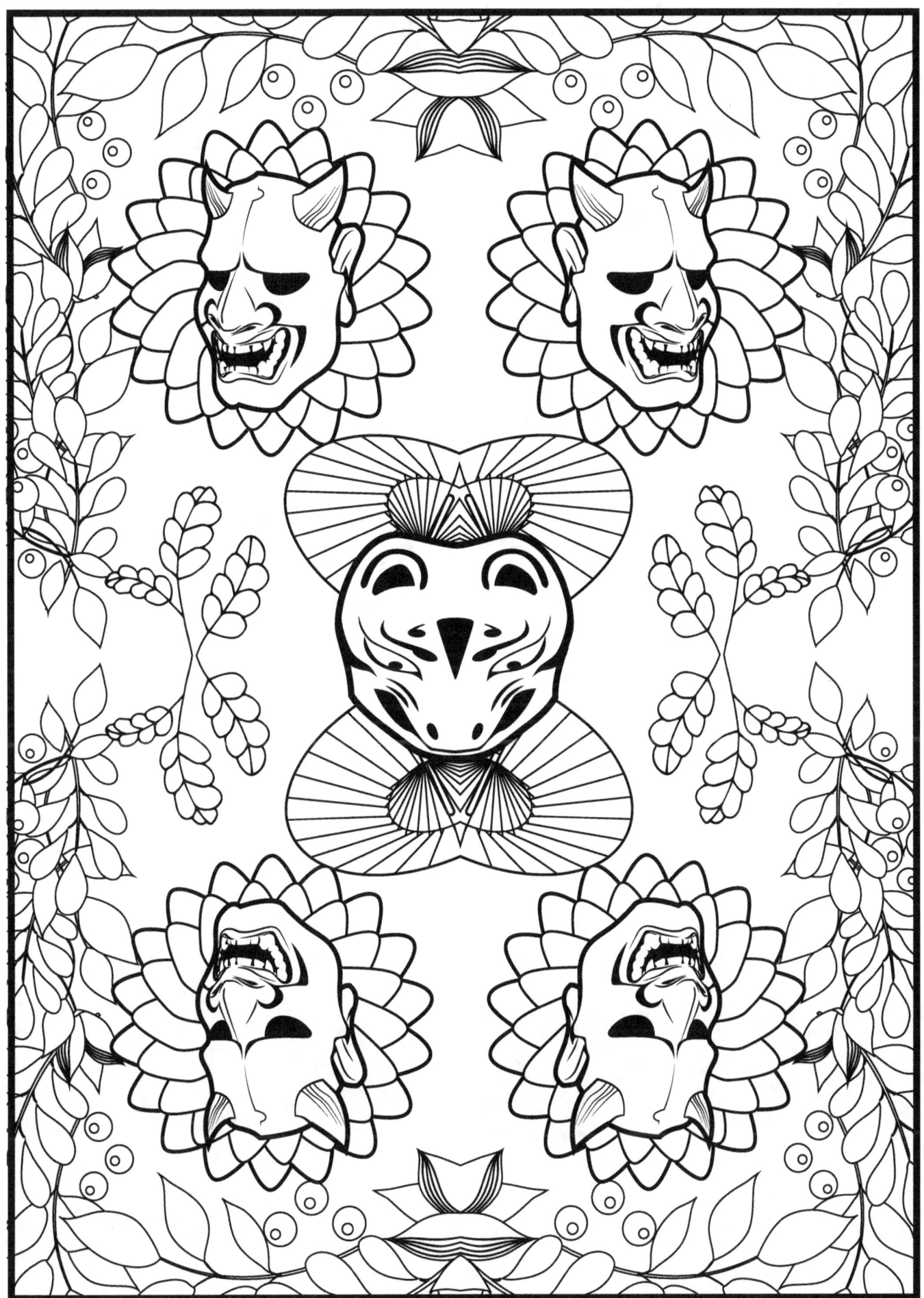

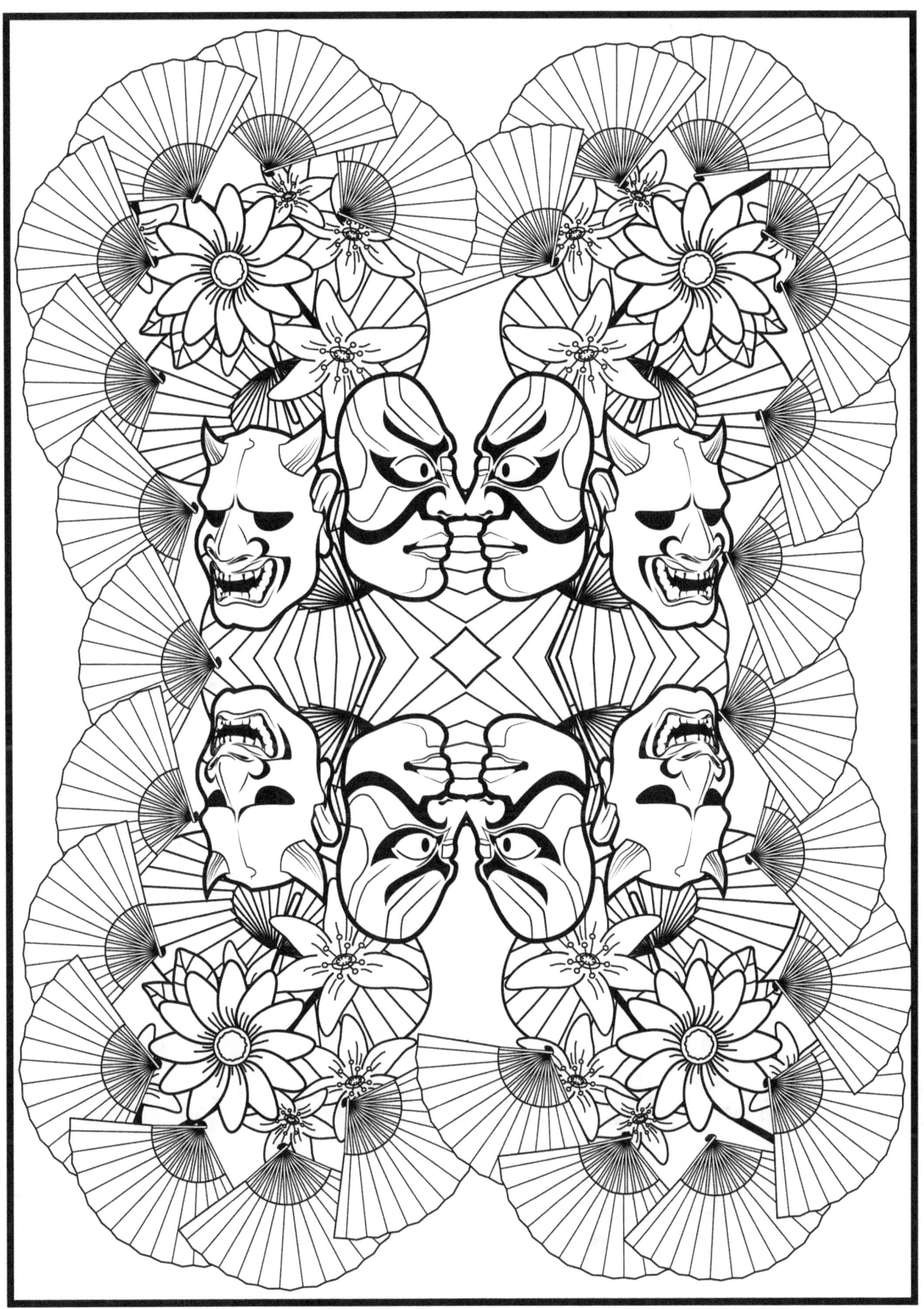

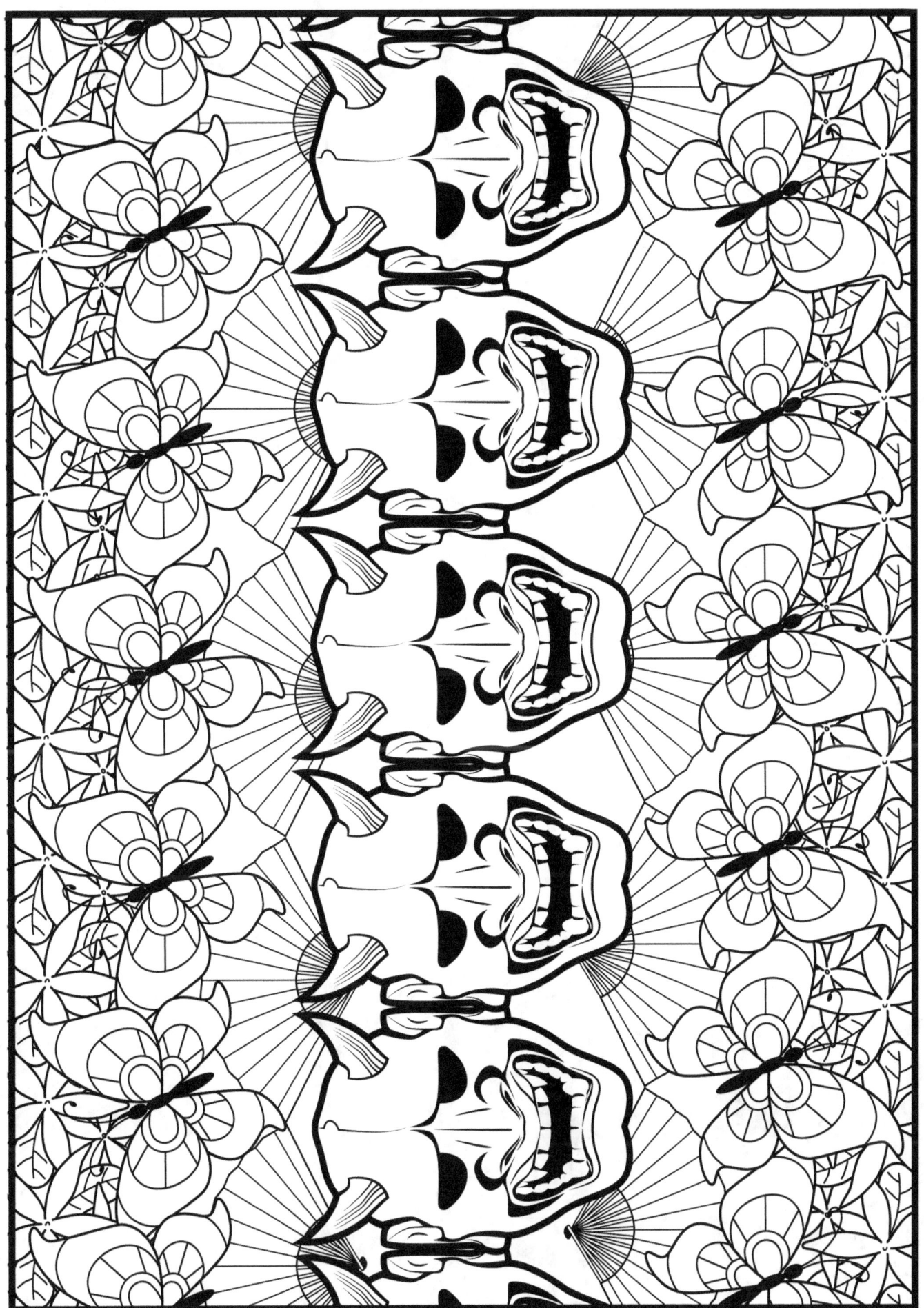

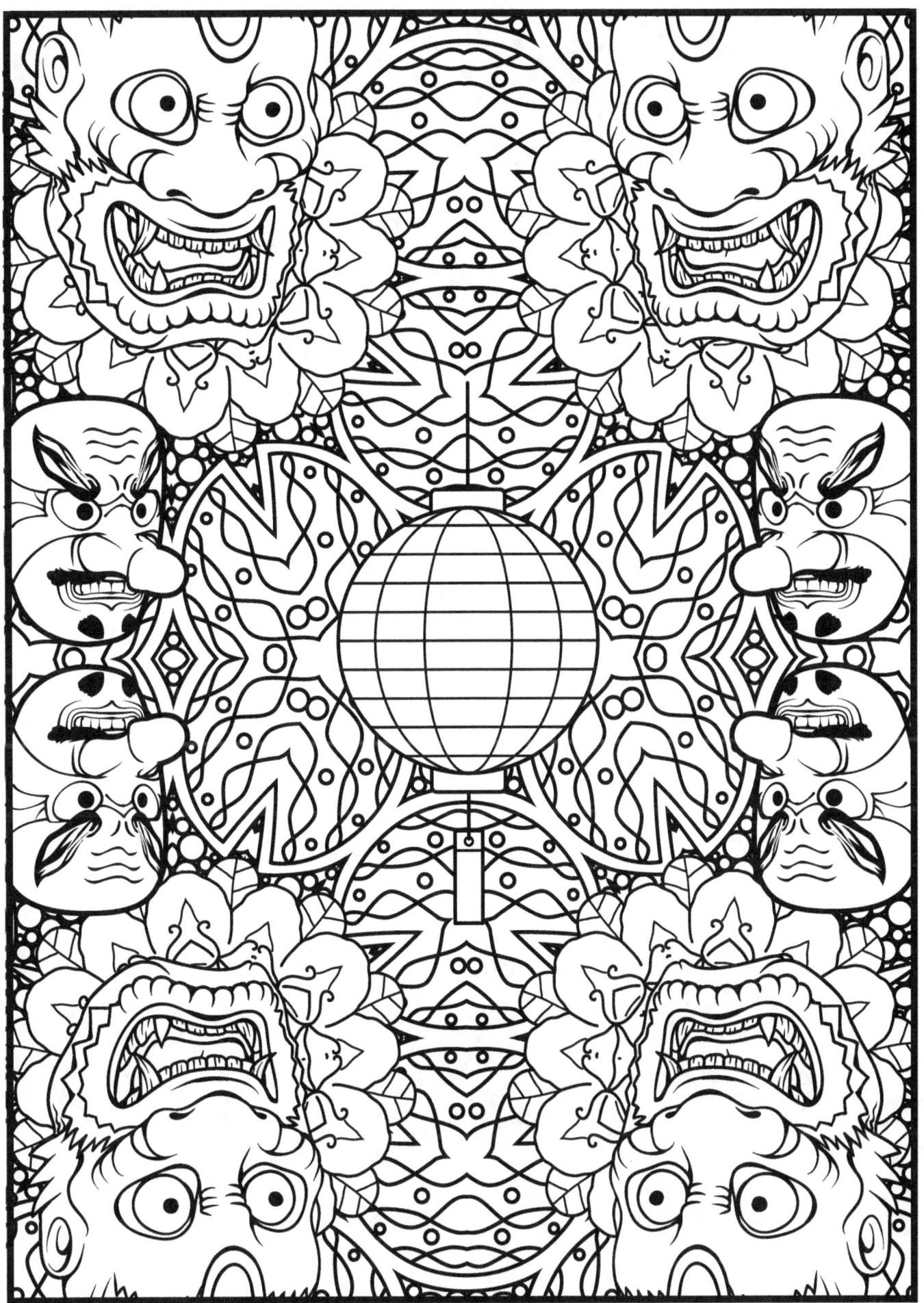

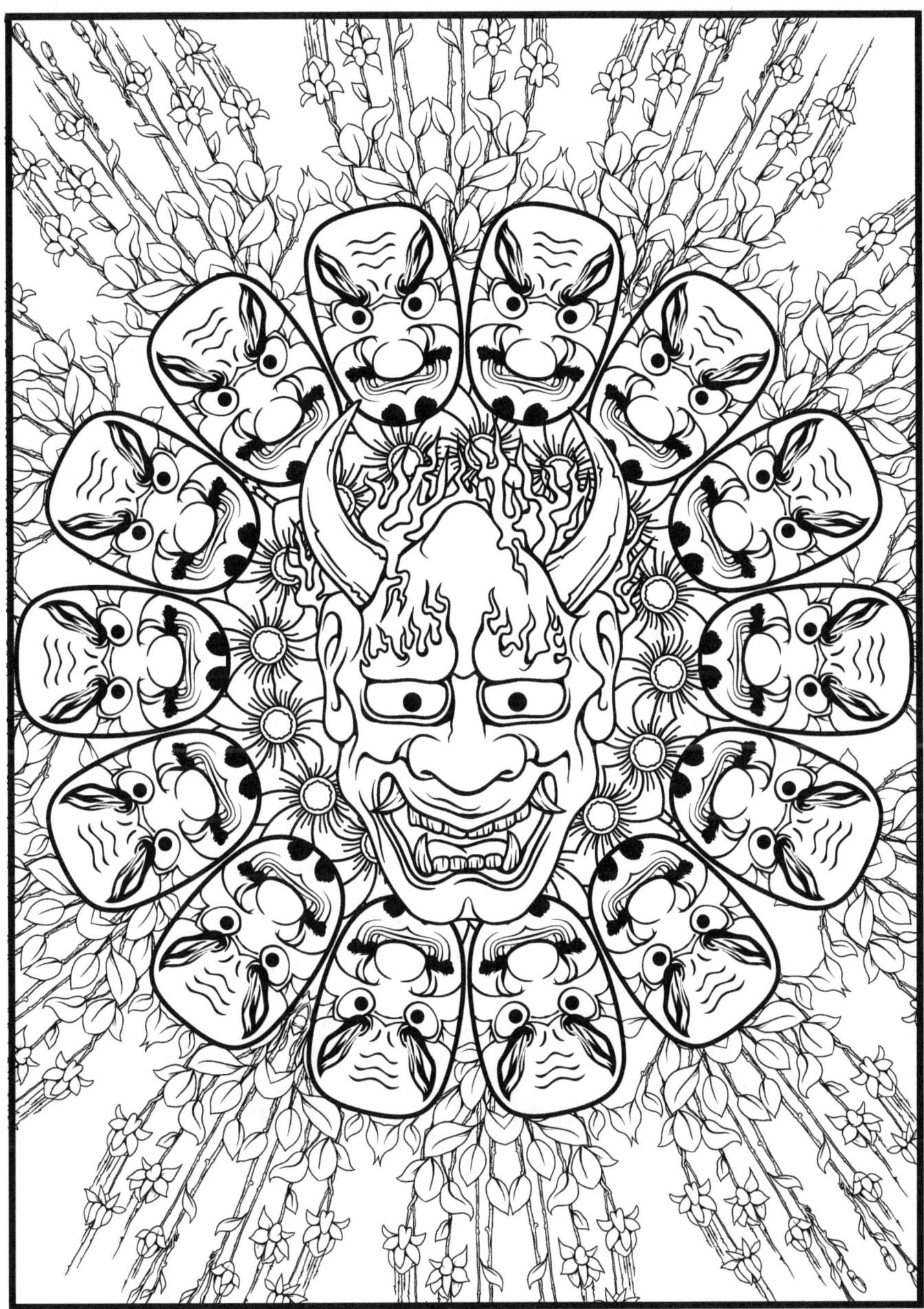

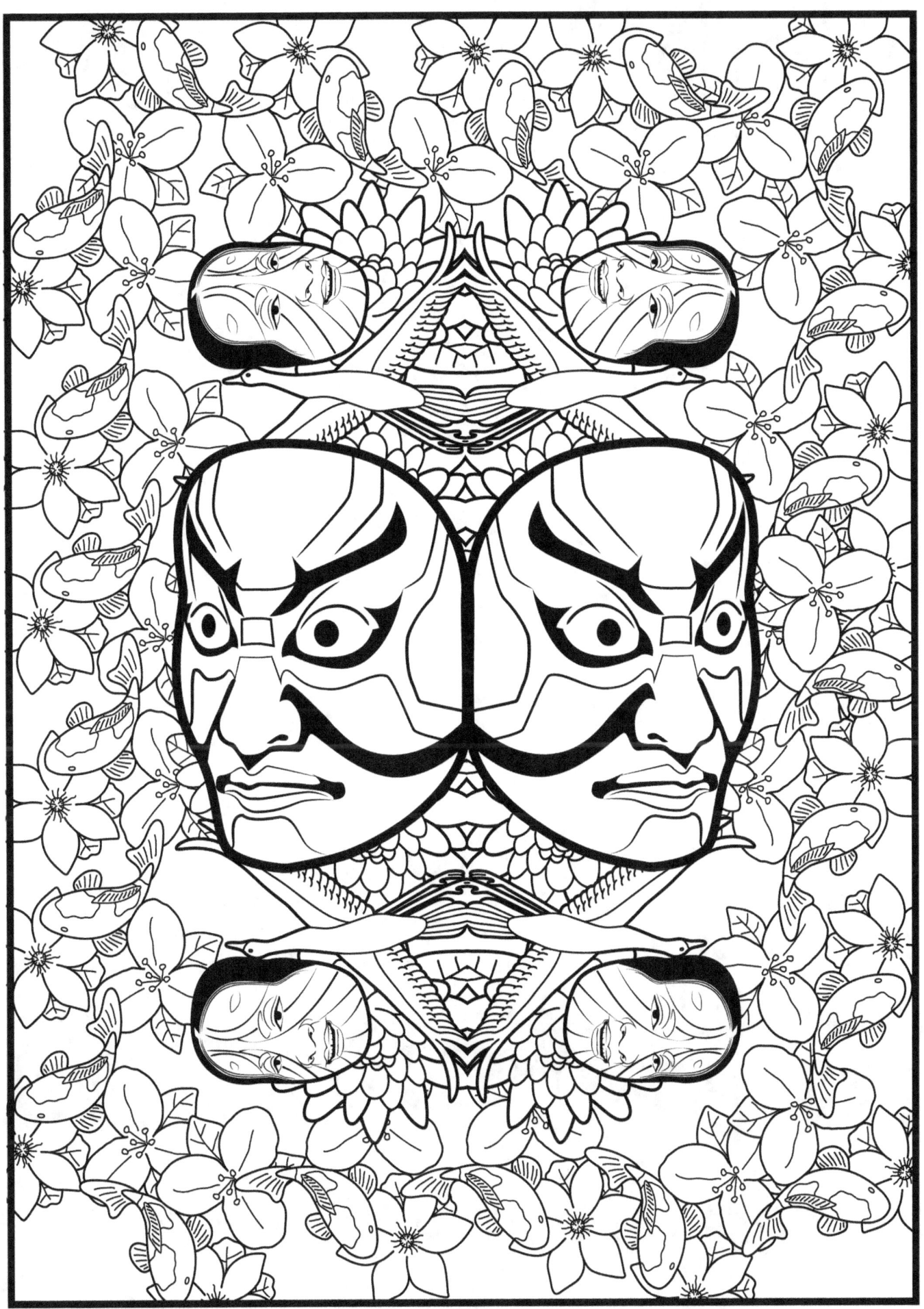

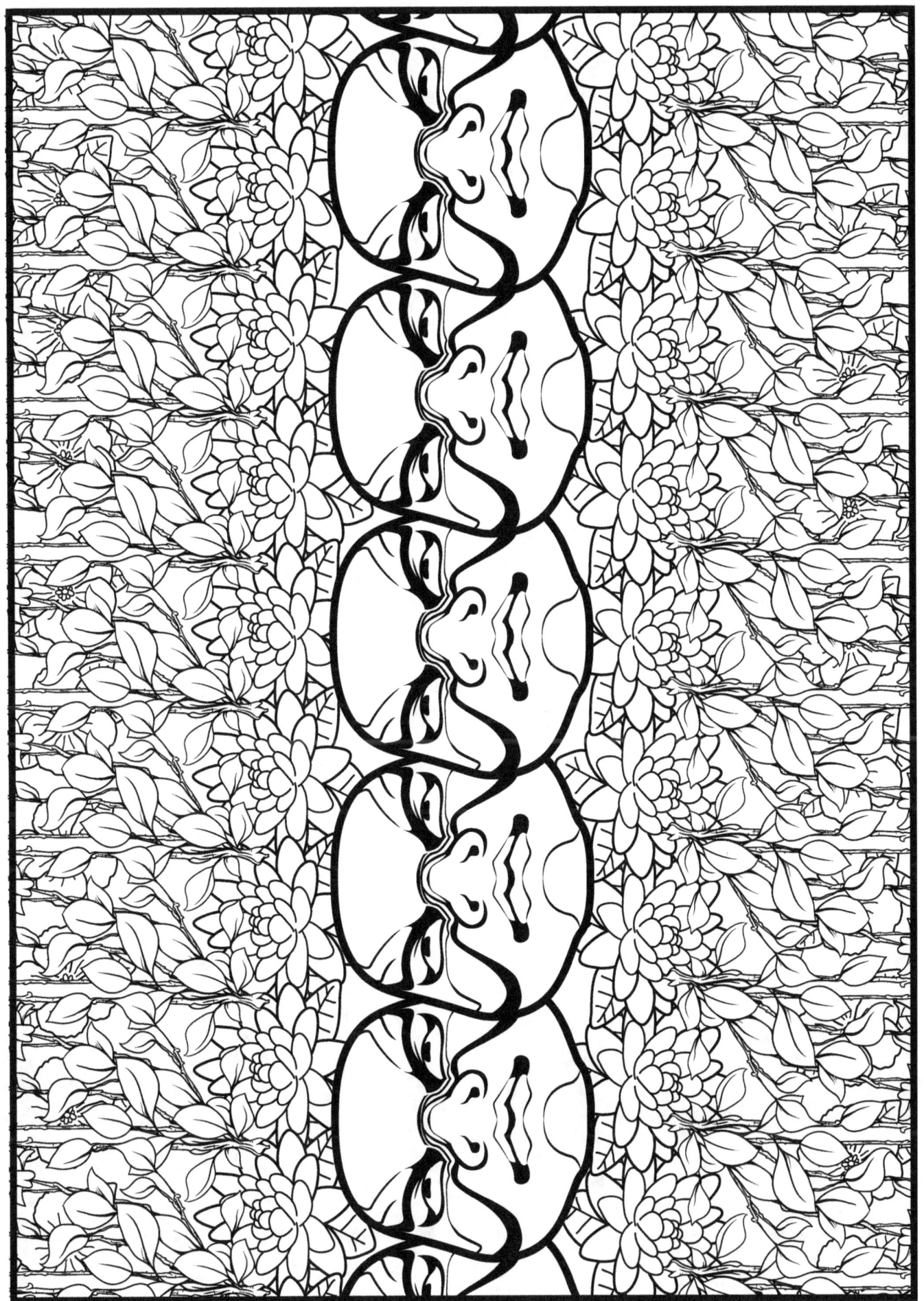

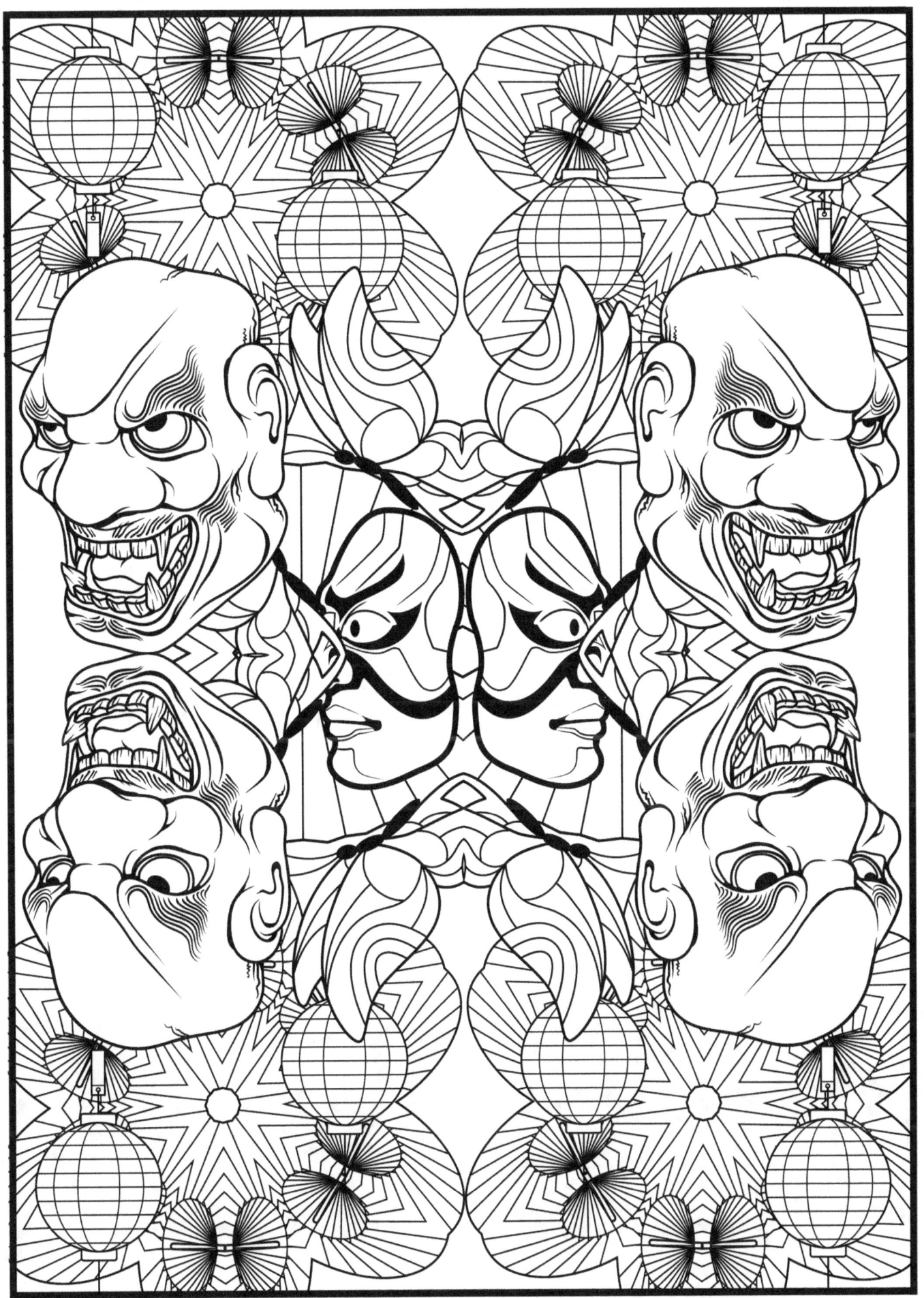

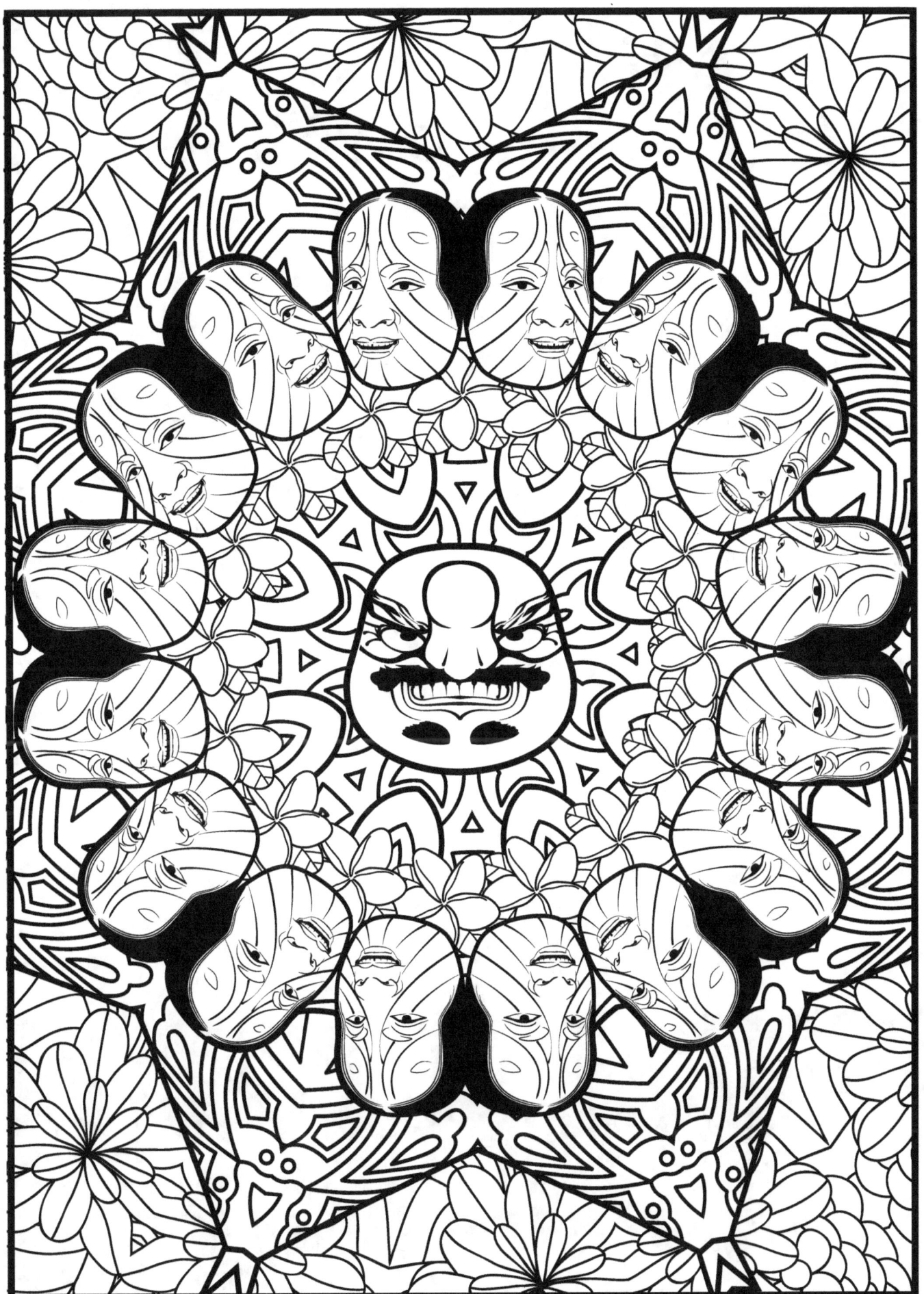

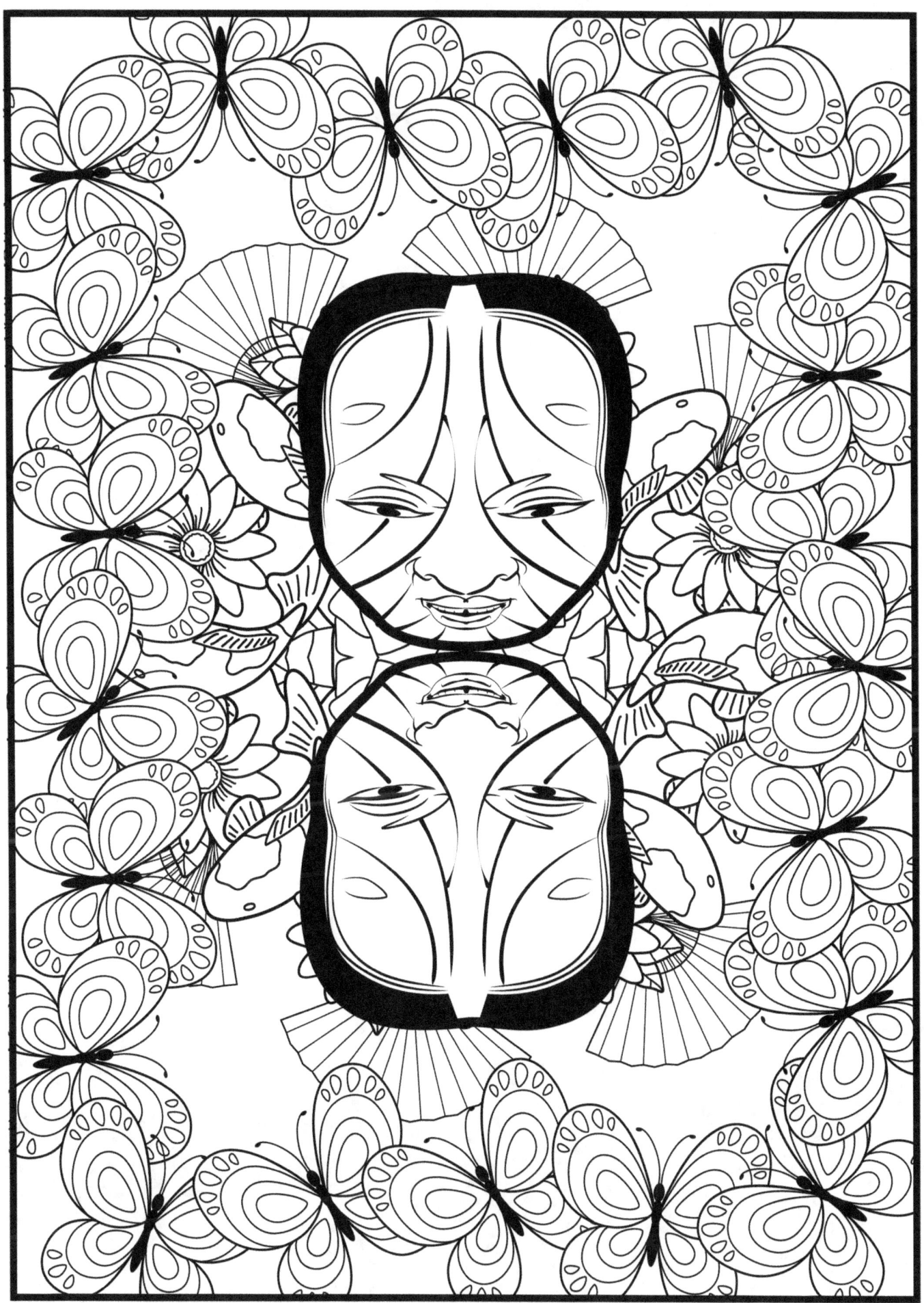

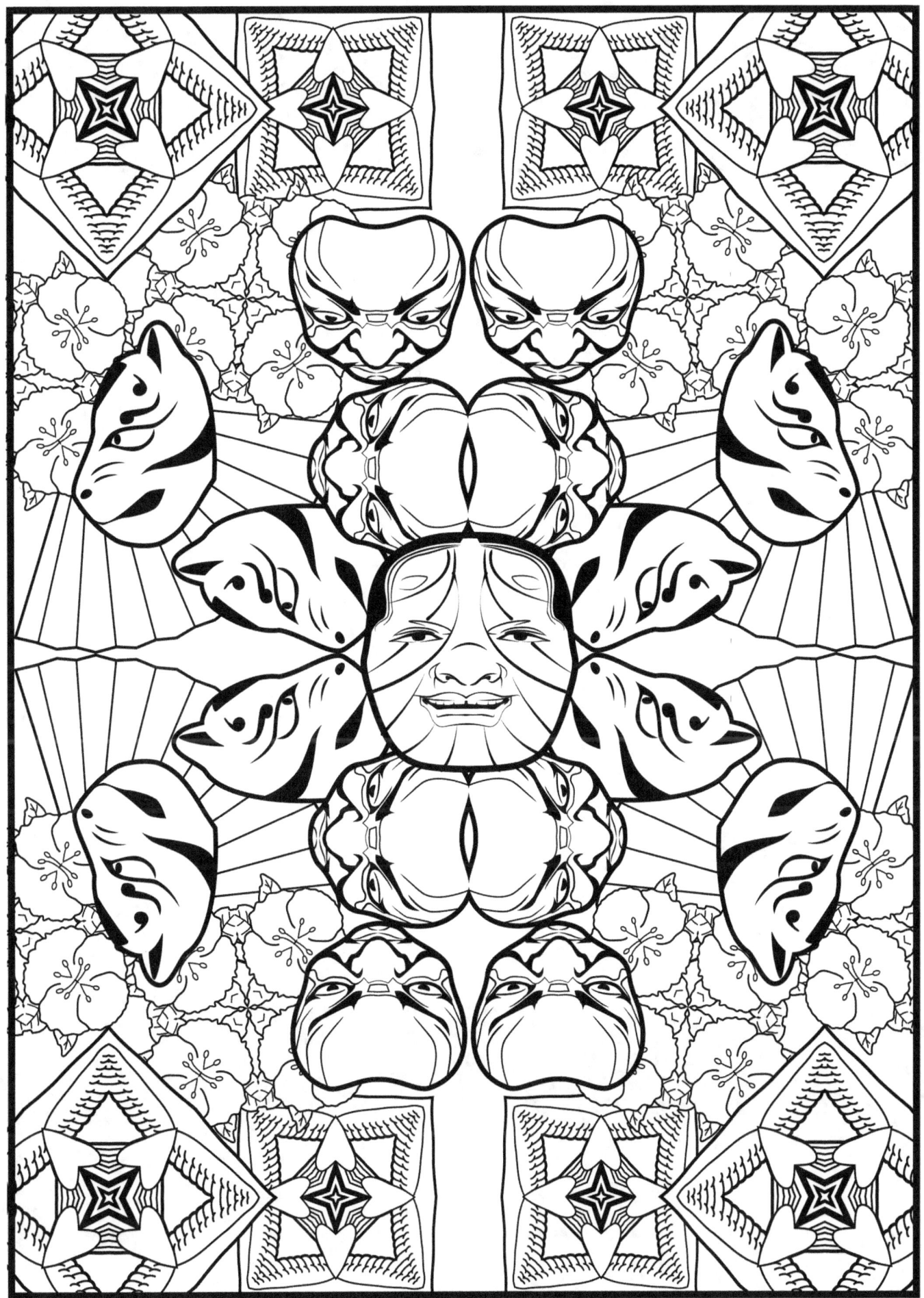

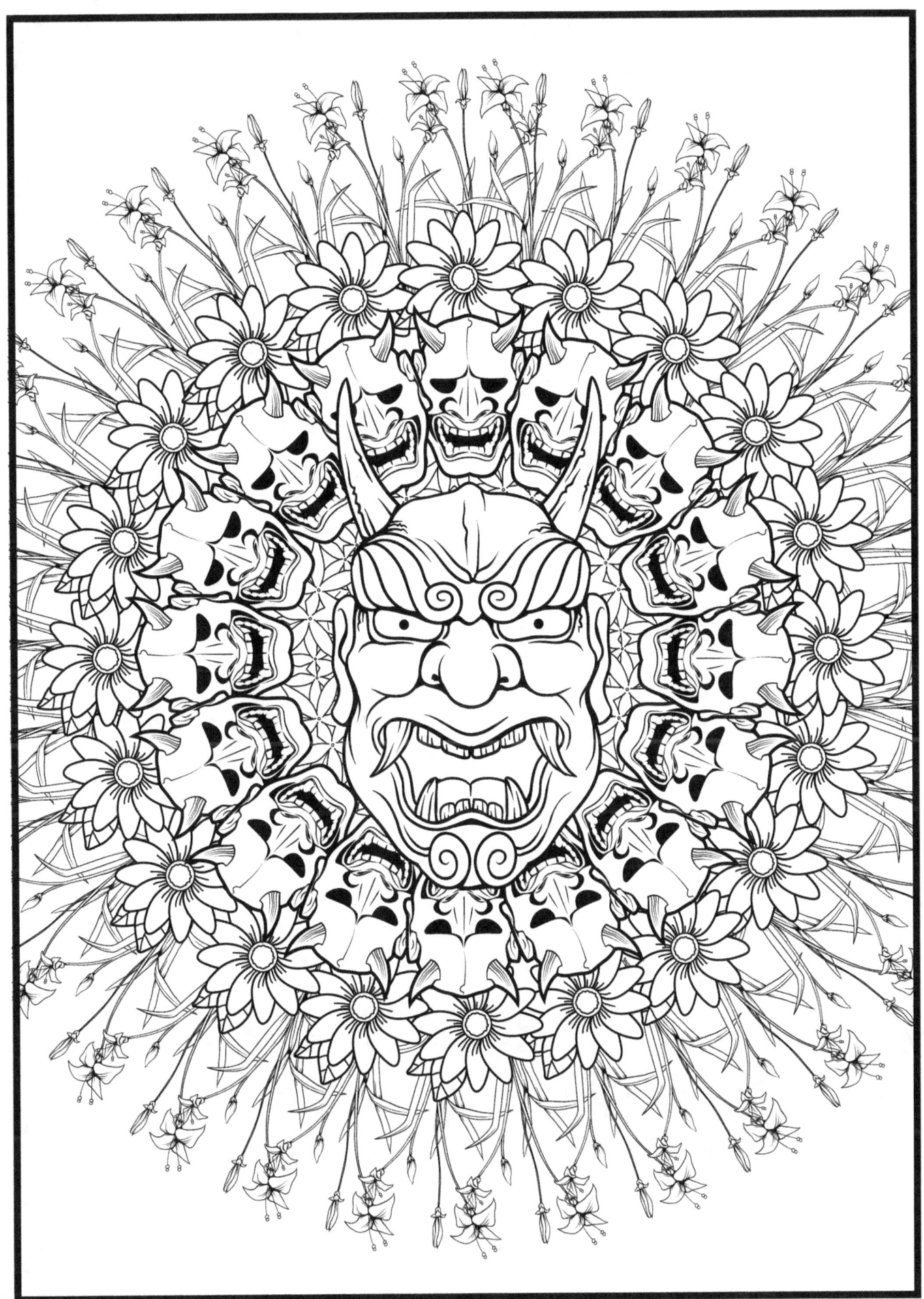

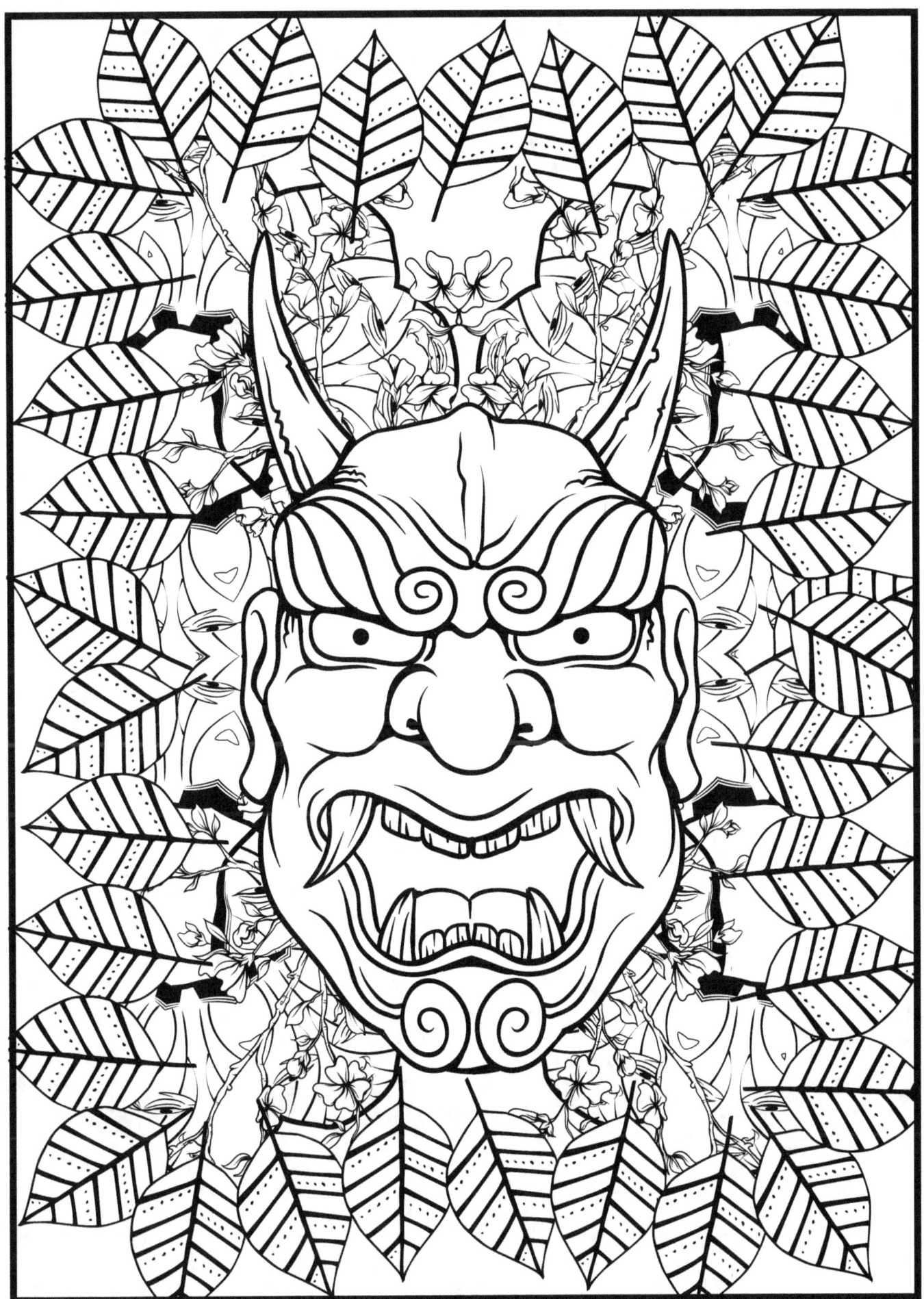

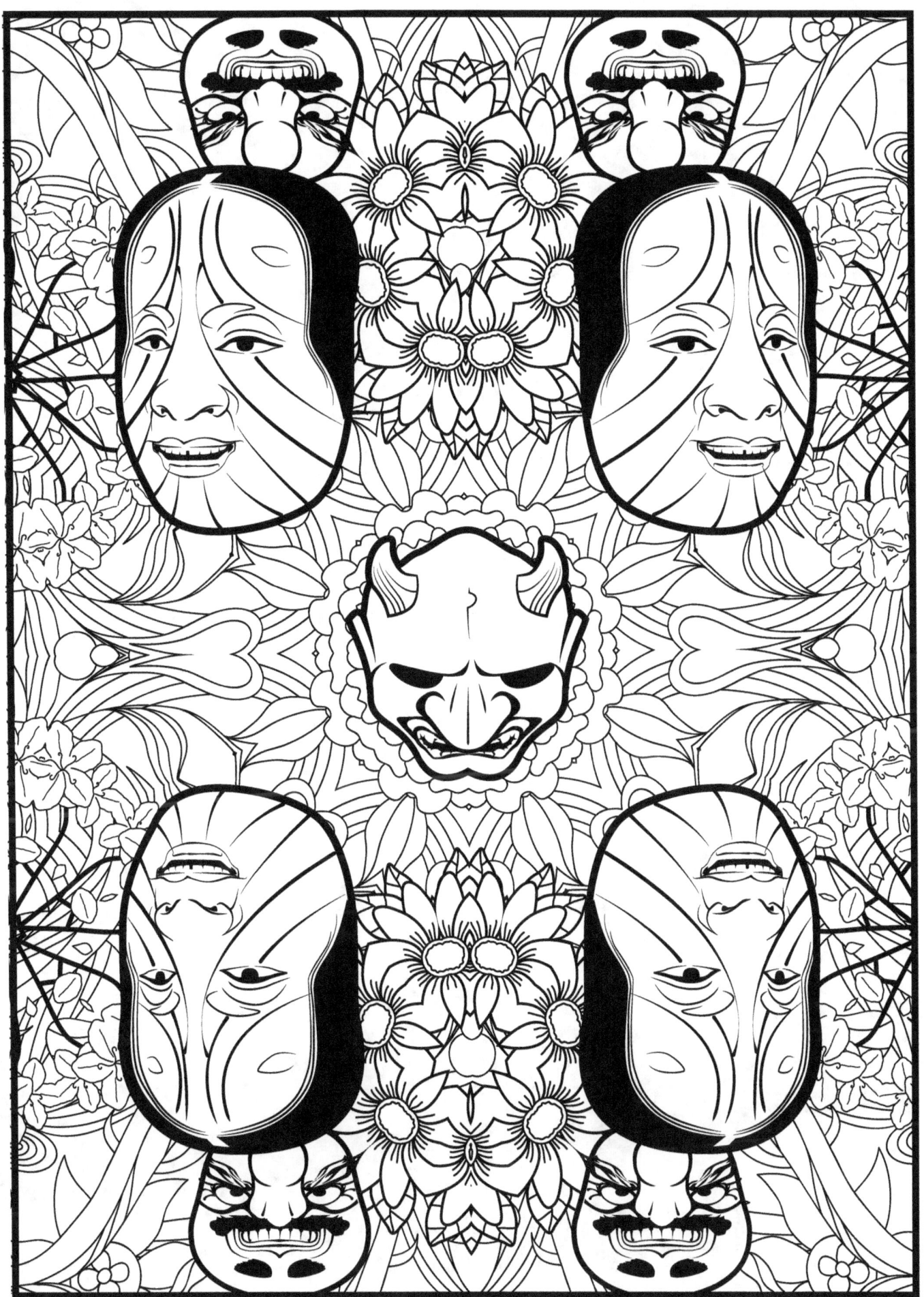

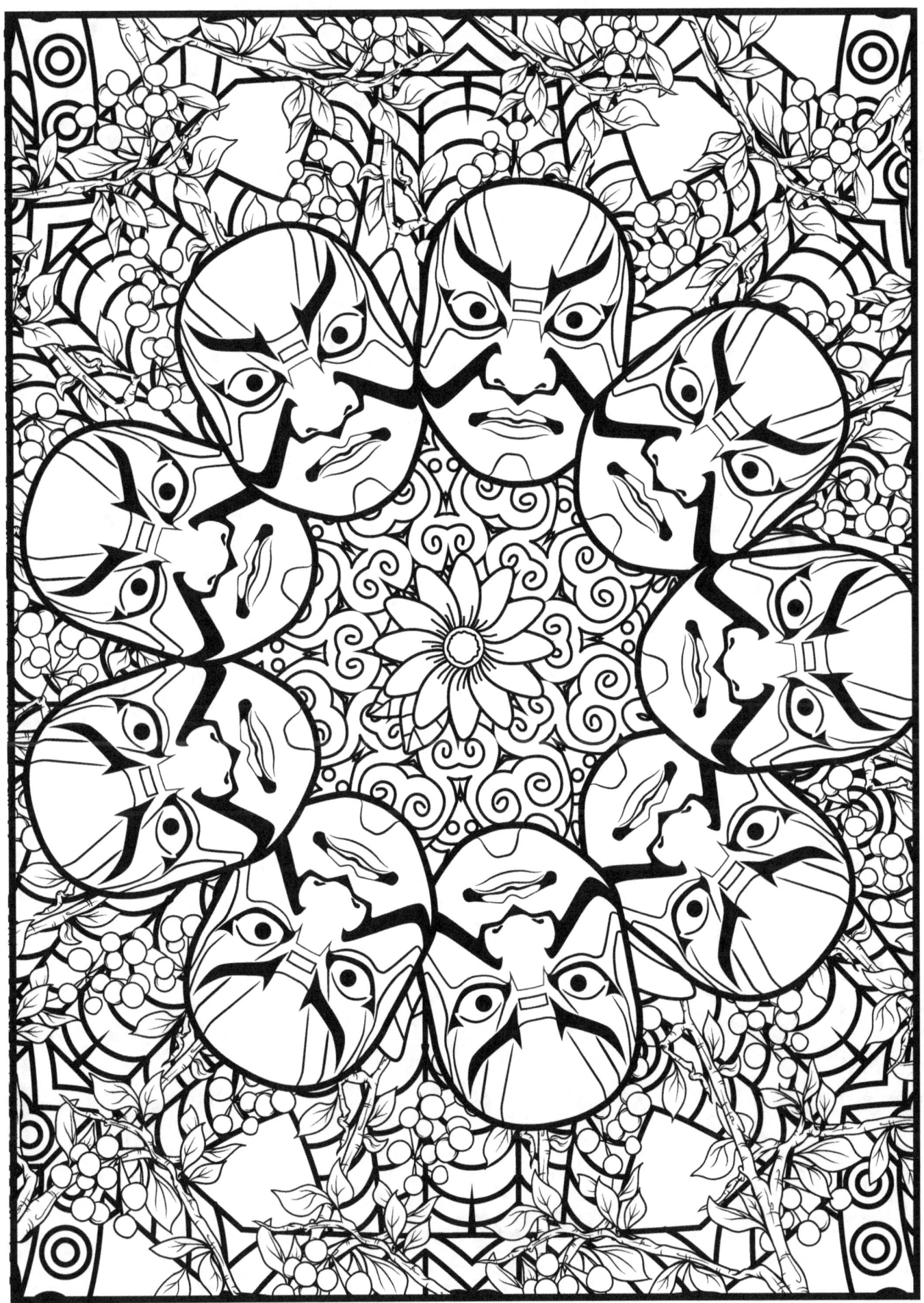